Dream College Admissions
Made Possible

From My Family To Yours

Tried and True Tips

For Parents/Students

in Middle/High School

Peter YZ Jiang. MD. PhD

First edition available in eBook, January 2013, and in print, March 2013

ISBN-13: 978-1477591079

Publisher: CreateSpace, a company of Amazon.com

Printed in the USA

1.   Education – home school. 2. College admission – tips. 3. College application – counseling. I. Title

Dedicated to my family

in America

and

in China

Table of Contents

Preface

Chapter 1. The big, the new and the little Ivy League colleges and the college planning time table.....1

Chapter 2. Class rank and GPA.....16

Chapter 3. SAT I and II scores (PSAT and ACT).....26

Chapter 4. AP and IB scores and current courses.....47

Chapter 5. Honors and awards.....51

Chapter 6. Extracurricular activities.....55

Chapter 7. The long and short college essays.....71

Chapter 8. Recommendation letters.....93

Chapter 9. The role of a private college counselor.....96

Chapter 10. Which colleges to visit or apply to?.....103

Chapter 11. Final packaging and sample student profiles.....112

Chapter 12. The alumni interview and the waiting list.....137

Chapter 13. Sending students off to college.....153

Chapter 14. Facts and fictions on the value of college education.....181

After Words.....202

References......205

Appendix 1. The Common Application Form - detailed version 206

Appendix 2. The college planning and application time table for parents and
            students.....216

Appendix 3. The 51 tips in Dream College Admissions Made Possible.....219

Appendix 4. About the author.....223

Preface

Most parents dream of their children getting into a top college. But how do they make the dream come true? Is there a "silver bullet" that gives students a sure shot at an "Ivy League" college or one of equal caliber? What can parents do to help their children reach this goal?

Many of our family friends asked June (my wife) and me these questions when our first son, Lauda (not his real name; real names withheld in this book for privacy), attended Stanford University in California. He was also accepted to Pomona College, the University of Pennsylvania, and others. We had ideas, but not definitive answers.

When our second son, Shaudi, was accepted by Pomona College in California, as well as Cornell University and others, more friends came to us with the same questions. Did we, as parents, do something right? Two students from the same family earning entry to top colleges hardly make a statistical certainty. Had we had a third child who made it to an Ivy League college, we might make a claim for extraordinary success in parenting. However, the "third student" in the family is our goldendoodle, Lisi. Though Lisi did have some obedience schooling, she is unlikely to improve our collegiate parenting credentials.

We do know one thing for certain: both Lauda and Shaudi worked hard during their public school career. It was they who made the grades and earned the achievements. For those years, their school work, activities, and life were the center of our family life. Their successes were a top priority for us as parents. During their formative years, we knew our children better than they knew themselves. Our observations of them and our work at home in raising them may shed some light on the process for other parents.

It's true there is no set of rules and there are no formulas for success in parenting. No two children are the same, and ours could not be more different from each other. In sharing lessons via family memoir, though, we hope readers, our fellow parents, will gain inspiration from our successes or draw some lessons from our failures. Of our close family friends who have followed our advice, already, several parents have seen their children accepted into highly selective colleges.

To raise an "Ivy League student," there is a package of demanding tasks for parents along with a long, tortuous 18-year journey. Parents begin as protectors of helpless infants. They then become guardians of youngsters, guides of elementary-age students, and champions and chauffeurs of middle school students. The relationship then turns, as parents become "enemies" or "most hated" people to teenagers. Finally, parents alternate between being the drill sergeants and the champions of high school students before sending their almost-adult to college.

Giving birth is hard, but it is no easier to raise a well-rounded child to become a successful adult.

Both June and I are first-generation immigrants to the United States. We did not have formal classroom experience in this country. It took us many years of trial and error to navigate the American educational system. If our children can do it, so can any student in America. It is our sincere hope that our reflections provide some guidance for all present and future parents in preparing children for their dream colleges.

Chapter 1. The big, the new, and the little Ivy League colleges and a college planning timetable

1.1. A brief history of American colleges

Since Harvard College opened its doors in 1636 to nine students, colleges and universities have mushroomed in the United States. The Carnegie Foundation's "Classification of Institutions of Higher Learning," in 2010, estimated the country held more than 4,600 institutions of higher learning offering one kind of degree or another. With this growth over the centuries, American universities have gained preeminence in higher education around the world. The inventions and contributions to mankind made by faculty and students at American universities have no match around the globe.

That also means America has the most desired colleges of any able student and scholar in the world. In working to gain college or university admission, then, American high school students don't only face competition from their peers in other States, they also face competition from their peers in other countries.

There are good reasons for this attraction to an American education. A 2012 study conducted by the Times Higher Education Group ranked 400 of the top universities around the world. Of the top 20, 15 were in the United States (*www.timeshighereducation.co.uk/world-university-rankings*). The ranking has historical confirmation. Since the 1930s, about 60 percent of all Nobel Prize winners resided in American higher education or research institutions[1].

Simply put: getting into a top, American college equals an opportunity for education at the top of the world.

This is why many parents dream of an "Ivy League college education" for their children. But what, exactly, is an Ivy League college education? Are other universities or colleges just as good?

The term "Ivy League" was originally used to denote a group of colleges in an athletic conference in the Northeast region of the United States. The term became official after formation of the National Collegiate Athletic Association (NCAA) Division I athletic conference in 1954. The Ivy League comprises eight private institutions of higher education. Still all in the Northeastern United States, these schools are some of the oldest educational institutions founded in the United States. In fact, seven of the eight private colleges were founded during the United States colonial period, before the American Revolution and the birth of the nation.

The Ivy League colleges and their locations, listed by year founded:

Institution	Founded
Harvard University, Cambridge, MA	1636 as New College
Yale University, New Haven, CT	1701 as Collegiate School
University of Pennsylvania, Philadelphia, PA	1740 as Church and Charity School of Philadelphia
Princeton University, Princeton, NJ	1746 as College of New Jersey
Columbia University,	1754 as King's College

New York, NY	
Brown University, Providence, RI	1764 as the College in the English Colony of Rhode Island and Providence Plantations
Dartmouth College, Hanover, NH	1769
Cornell University, Ithaca, NY	1865

Today, however, the phrase is no longer limited to athletics. Now, "Ivy League" connotes standards of academic excellence, admissions selectivity, and social elitism. In addition, Ivy League schools are often viewed by the public as some of the most prestigious, and the schools are often ranked among the best universities in the United States and worldwide. Undergraduate enrollments among the Ivy League schools range from about 4,000 to 14,000. This makes the student body at Ivy League schools larger than those at a typical private liberal arts college, but smaller than those at a typical public state university.

But the Ivy League is not alone in offering a great education. The northeast region was one of the first to be settled in America, so the Ivy League does have a claim on maturity. But, over the centuries, as the population migrated south, inland, and to the West Coast, hundreds of new universities and colleges opened to students. Some of the newer colleges have gained prestige and superiority in academic performance and contributions to mankind, especially in the fields of electrical engineering and biotechnology. Some people call these colleges and universities the "New Ivy League." The list of the "New Ivy League" colleges varies from source to source. However, based on my research, some names in the "New Ivy League" come up more frequently and consistently.

3

The "New Ivy League" colleges and their locations, listed by year founded and denoting public/private status:

Institution	Founded
Duke University, Durham, NC	1838, private
Northwestern University, Evanston, IL	1851, private
Washington University at St. Louis, St. Louis, MO	1853, private
Massachusetts Institute of Technology, Cambridge, MA	1861, private
University of California-Berkeley, Berkeley, CA	1868, public
Johns Hopkins University, Baltimore, MD	1876, private
Stanford University, Stanford, CA	1891, private
California Institute of Technology, Pasadena, CA	1891, private
University of Chicago, Chicago, IL	1892, private

But there is yet another group of fine colleges to compete with the original Ivy League and the New Ivy League. Some people refer to these colleges as the "American Hidden Secret" in higher education. These are the liberal arts colleges.

Liberal arts colleges do not have NCAA Division I teams, and thus are not well-known to the general public. A liberal arts college is one with a primary emphasis on undergraduate study in the liberal arts and sciences. Students generally major in a particular discipline while receiving exposure to a wide range of academic subjects, including sciences as well as traditional humanities subjects such as history, language, and philosophy.

The "liberal arts college experience" in the United States is characterized by three main aspects:

1. A smaller size than universities, which usually means more individual attention for each student.
2. A residential environment, which means students live and learn away from home, often for the first time, and must learn to live well with others. Additionally, the residential experience of living on campus brings a variety of cultural, political, and intellectual events to students who might not otherwise seek them out.
3. A typically two-year exploration of the liberal arts or general knowledge before declaring a major.

For some people, colleges without familiar names are not enough to satisfy their ego. But, to gain the true value of a higher education, these colleges are hidden secrets. Their selectivity in admissions, their often-long and rich histories, and their graduates' admirable career prospects can rival, if not supersede, some of the "original" and the "new" Ivy League colleges. It's no surprise some people call the top-ranked liberal arts colleges the "Little Ivy League."

The "Little Ivy League" colleges and their locations, listed by year founded and denoting public/private status:

Institution	Founded
Williams College, Williamstown, MA	1793, private
Bowdoin College, Brunswick, ME	1794, private
Middlebury College, Middlebury, VT	1800, private
Amherst College, Amherst, MA	1821, private
Haverford College, Haverford, PA	1833, private
Swarthmore College, Swarthmore, PA	1864, private
Carleton College, Northfield, MN	1866, private
Wellesley College, Wellesley, MA	1870, private
Pomona College, Claremont, CA	1887, private

Claremont McKenna College, Claremont, CA	1946, private

Many other institutions, including Carnegie Mellon, Emory University, the University of California-Los Angeles, the University of Michigan-Ann Arbor, the University of North Carolina-Chapel Hill, the University of Virginia, Vanderbilt University, Brandeis University, and Tufts University, may be equally prestigious and competitive. Additionally, certain schools not considered among the Ivy or the "New Ivy" leagues may have a specific program superior to any of those listed above, yet the school itself may not be ranked because distinction in a particular area is usually not included in a school's general ranking. Examples of such programs include The New School (formerly, The New School for Social Research), where the avant-garde curriculum excels in preparing students for rigorous graduate programs, particularly in the social and political sciences. The University of Connecticut has the distinction of providing more successful applicants to highly competitive veterinary science graduate programs than almost any other school in the country. The University of Miami is world-famous for its marine science program at the Rosenstiel School of Marine Biology and Atmospheric Science. The list goes on.

Clearly, there are many fine colleges and universities in the United States. But, for some parents, only the top will do, and that means an Ivy League or Ivy-like education. This book is for them.

1.2. The college application and college planning timetable

Unlike the admission process in China, where June and I attended college and higher education was decided by a single test score, the admission process in the

United States is more complicated. Many factors are at play, both subjective and objective. The following chapters will help students and parents navigate the application process. The book contents follow the sequence of items as they appear on the Common Application Form for colleges and universities.

More than 400 four-year colleges now accept a student's Common Application Form via the internet (www.commonapp.org). For modern students or parents with basic internet familiarity, setting up an account is simple. After the first three pages, which ask for student demographics and identification, come pages asking for various facts and scores. These pages may take considerable time to complete. The facts and scores section requires an in-depth, detailed accounting of years of a student's scholastic output and extracurricular activities. Then, after completing common requirements, the student must write short essays and answer questions, called supplementary information, which are specifically requested by individual colleges. By this point, the application is almost done. But it takes a lot of work to get to that point.

A detailed version of the Common Application Form can be found in Appendix 1. Shown here is an abbreviated version with the categorical headings only.

© 2011 The Common Application, Inc.	2011-12 First-year Application
	For Spring 2012 or Fall 2012 Enrollment

APPLICANT

Legal Name_____

FUTURE PLANS

College _____ Deadline _____

Decision Plan_____

Academic Interests _____

Career Interest_____

DEMOGRAPHICS

Citizenship Status _____

Non-US Citizenship _____

FAMILY

Legal Guardian (if other than a parent)

Siblings

Parent 1: _ Mother _ Father _ Unknown

Parent 2: _ Mother _ Father _ Unknown

EDUCATION

Secondary Schools

School Name & CEEB/ACT Code Location (City, State/Province, ZIP/Postal Code, Country)

ACADEMICS

The self-reported information in this section is not intended to take the place of your official records. Please note the requirements of each institution to which you are applying and arrange for official transcripts and score reports to be sent from your secondary school and the appropriate testing agencies. Where "Best Scores" are requested, please report the highest individual scores you have earned so far, even if those scores are from different test dates.

Grades: Class Rank _____ Class Size ____ Weighted? _ Yes _ No

GPA _____Scale _____ Weighted? _ Yes _ No

ACT Exam Dates: _____ Best Scores: _____ _____

SAT Exam Dates: _____ Best Scores: ___ _____

TOEFL/IELTS Exam Dates: _____Best Score: ____ ___ _____

AP/IB

Subjects   Best Scores: _____

Current Courses Please indicate title, level (AP, IB, advanced honors, etc.) and credit value of all courses you are taking this year. Indicate quarter classes taken in the same semester on the appropriate semester line.

Honors Briefly list any academic distinctions or honors you have received since the 9th grade or international equivalent (e.g., National Merit, Cum Laude Society).

S(School) S/R(State or Regional N(National) I(International)

EXTRACURRICULAR ACTIVITIES & WORK EXPERIENCE

Extracurricular Please list your principal extracurricular, volunteer, and work activities in their order of importance to you. Feel free to group your activities and paid work experience separately if you prefer. Use the space available to provide details of your activities and accomplishments (specific events, varsity letter, musical instrument, employer, etc.). To allow us to focus on the highlights of your activities, please complete this section even if you plan to attach a résumé.

WRITING

Please briefly elaborate on one of your extracurricular activities or work experiences in the space below.

_____

Please write an essay of 250 – 500 words on a topic of your choice or on one of the options listed below, and attach it to your application before submission. Please indicate your topic by checking the appropriate box. This personal essay helps us become acquainted with you as a person and student, apart from courses, grades, test scores, and other objective data. It will also demonstrate your ability to organize your thoughts and express yourself. *NOTE: Your Common Application essay should be the same for all colleges. Do not customize it in any way for individual colleges. Colleges that want customized essay responses will ask for them on*

a supplement form.

_ _ Evaluate a significant experience, achievement, risk you have taken, or ethical dilemma you have faced and its impact on you.

_ _ Discuss some issue of personal, local, national, or international concern and its importance to you.

_ _ Indicate a person who has had a significant influence on you, and describe that influence.

_ _ Describe a character in fiction, a historical figure, or a creative work (as in art, music, science, etc.) that has had an influence on you, and explain that influence.

_ _ A range of academic interests, personal perspectives, and life experiences adds much to the educational mix. Given your personal background, describe an experience that illustrates what you would bring to the diversity in a college community or an encounter that demonstrated the importance of diversity to you.

_ _ Topic of your choice.

SIGNATURE

I affirm that I will send an enrollment deposit (or equivalent) to only one institution; sending multiple deposits (or equivalent) may result in the withdrawal of my admission offers from all institutions. [Note: students may send an enrollment deposit (or equivalent) to a second institution where they have been admitted from the waitlist, provided that they inform the first institution that they will no longer be enrolling.]

Signature _____

Date _____

Common Application member institution admission offices do not discriminate on the basis of race, color, ethnicity, national origin, religion, creed, sex, age, marital status, parental status, physical disability, learning disability, political affiliation, veteran status, or sexual orientation.

From reviewing the form, it is obvious that college planning should actually start early in a student's life. For instance during preschool and elementary school, parents should focus on fostering good learning habits, a fondness for reading books, and a passion for varieties of sports or artistic activities. From middle school onward, the strategy shifts to every activities to enhance the student's high school performance. We followed the timetable below starting when our sons were in middle school.

College Planning and Application Timetable: *A reference for parents and students.*

Grade Level	Extracurricular Activities	Goal
Before 5th	1. Cultivate interests in books and good study habit 2. Set limits on playtime 3. Try varieties of activities: arts, sports, music, et al	1. A good study habit goes for a life time 2. Learn parental expectations 3. Find out where the interest and talent lays
7th - 8th	1. Sports, arts — narrow down to one each. 2. Prepare for and take the real SAT I or ACT for practice	1. Join a team, club or arts group 2. Participate in university sponsored summer camps
9th - 10th	1. Sports, arts – join school team or group 2. Volunteer, in or out of school	1. Earn a team leadership position 2. Earn an official position in a club

	3. Spend summers on domestic or international volunteer work 4. Prepare for PSAT and SAT I	3. Accumulate hours and collect material for college essays 4. Ace PSAT to qualify to be a National Merit Scholar semi-finalist.
11th 1st semester (Fall and Winter)	1. Sports, arts – continue school team or group 2. Volunteer, in or out of school 3. Take the real PSAT 4. SAT I preparation: class or self-study 5. SAT II preparation: class or self-study.	1. Continue team leadership position 2. Continue club official position 3. Accumulate hours and collect material for college essay 4. Write an essay to compete to be a National Merit Scholar finalist 5. Ace SAT I on the first attempt 6. Ace SAT II on the first attempt
11th 2nd semester (Spring)	1. Sports, arts – continue school team or group 2. Volunteer, in or out of school 3. Take SAT I in April, May or June 4. Take the SAT II subject tests 5. Interview and find a private college counselor, if desired	1. Continue team leadership position 2. Continue club official position 3. Accumulate hours and collect material for college essay 4. If needed, make multiple test attempts for best combined score 5. Prepare for college application
Summer between 11th-12th	1. Draft long essay for college applications 2. Compile college list via online research 3. Continue summer volunteer work	1. Be prepared for a long haul 2. Sign up for fall season college campus tours 3. Spend three summers on the same activity; it shows compassion and perseverance.

12th (September, October, November)	1. Continue to retake SAT I or II if scores are not at desired level 2. Make college campus visits, if affordable 3. Ask teachers and counselors for recommendation letters (mid to late September) 4. Continue to work on the long essay for college applications 5. Get the class rank and GPA from the school counselor 6. Work on short college essay for the early decision or action college	1. SAT I total score should be at least 2200; SAT II should be at least 720 2. Narrow the list to nine colleges 3. Get favorite teachers' promises to write recommendations 4. Perfect the essay, after many edits 5. Set up application account via www.commonapp.org 6. Take early decision or early action decisions/options seriously
12th (December, January)	1. Meet deadlines: December 1 or January 1 for most early applications 2. Continue to work on short essays in case early application fails to secure an admission letter	1. Check college web site or email for announcement of early admission decisions
12th (January, February)	1. If early application failed, apply to other colleges. If it succeeded, pay the deposit and skip to activities for May, June. 2. Watch deadlines; each college requires materials by different dates and times	1. Choose three dream colleges; three reachable colleges and three safety colleges 2. Aim to submit applications one week before a deadline
12th (February, March)	1. Prepare for alumni interviews: research the college; be genuinely interested in the college 2. Monitor accounts at each college applied to for any missing document.	1. Connect well with the alumni interviewer to earn a glowing evaluation report 2. Submit any missing document promptly, incomplete files will not be read

12th (March, April)	1. Anxiously await good news; check email and regular mailbox 2. Provide supplemental information to waitlist colleges	1. Take action promptly, if waitlisted 2. Get off the waitlist to land a spot at a dream college
12th (April, May)	1. If unsure where to attend, revisit colleges that offered admission 2. Pay deposit to the best college	1. Select a final dream college to attend 2. College admission secured!
12th (May, June)	1. Celebrate successful high school life and parenting 2. Enjoy time with high school friends, as the group will soon be apart	1. Appreciate hard work – it pays off 2. Cultivate friendships, and continue loyalty to high school friends.
12th (July, August)	1. Shop for college-bound student 2. Choose 1st year courses in college	1. Ensure functional living away from home 2. Try to listen to parents.
12th (August, September)	1. Send student off to college 2. Reflect on college application journey.	1. Keep parental love active from afar 2. Treat parental "empty nest syndrome" 3. Help other parents achieve what you have done.

Chapter 2. Class Rank and GPA

The first two questions on the academic section of the application form ask for the student's class rank and GPA (grade point average). This prominence shows class rank and GPA are among the most influential factors to determine a student's chance to get into his or her dream college. After all, college is about education. It's fair for a student's academic strength to get priority.

But there are ways to improve these numbers that go beyond diligent studying. Class rank is generated by comparing the GPAs among the students in a grade cohort at a school. The student with the highest GPA will rank number one, the student with the second-highest GPA will rank number two, and so on.

The numbers can be complex, though. In addition to a simple calculation based on grades on a school transcript, there is also a weighted GPA and class rank. This weighted measure depends on the school's perceived difficulty of a student's courses. A student may earn a B+ in a difficult course, for example. But the final weighted GPA and class rank for the student who earned the B+ may be higher than those for a student who chose an easier, lower-level class and earned an A. Each high school has its own policy. Some do not rank at all. Others do not calculate weighted GPA or ranking. The parent or student should inquire about this policy at the school counselor's office.

June and I were naïve when Lauda was applying for college in 2006. We did not think much about class rank and GPA, since we never had such a grading system in China when we were in high school there. One late October day after he started his senior year, Lauda came home and told us he was ranked number one in his class. The school counselor just had given out the confidential class ranks to each of the graduating students so they could complete college application forms.

This is a typical way for students to learn their class rank. After all, class rank is not published. It is locked in the counselor's computer. A student or parents can ask the counselor for an updated class rank at any time. June and I knew Lauda was a strong student and had been getting straight A's and had a 4.0 GPA since entering 9th grade, but we did not expect the number one spot, nor did we comprehend its importance. In fact, just five months prior to that notice, we had to make up Lauda's class rank when we visited the college fair at our local convention center. At each exhibition desk, college representatives from all over the country welcomed each passing parent to fill out the student's information on a card. Since Lauda was not with us, we debated what number to write. We analyzed his strengths and put down number five.

In retrospect, Lauda deserved the first spot. He somehow knew the "tricks" to get to the top of the pack. For example, he had been taking Spanish class since the 7th grade. When he entered the 9th grade, his level was considered high school Spanish 200, thus by the 12th grade he was in Spanish 500, the highest possible class. Since this Spanish course was considered a high-level class, it carried more weight when counting Lauda's GPA and weighted class ranking. Most four-year colleges require at least two or three years of foreign language during high school. Had Lauda just satisfied the high school graduation and minimal college admission requirements and not progressed to 500, his weighted GPA and class rank would have been lower. Many of his classmates with whom he grew up did the same thing. But, for those who did not carry on to the 500 level, but instead stopped at 400 or 300, the GPA and class rank did not receive the benefit of the extra weight of the high-level class.

This same principle applies to other subjects in the high school curriculum. The tougher or higher level of the subject, the greater the reward. But, there is a balancing act here, too. If the student struggles with the high-level course and is on track to get a grade of a B or C, the family has two options. The parent may need to help the student identify and rectify an obstacle, thus enabling the student to earn a better grade in the higher class. Or, the student may need to move to a lower class so he or she may earn a higher grade. A persistent, lower grade in any subject is a red flag to college admissions officers.

Our local public high school is one of the few high schools in our state or even the country to offer mainly International Baccalaureate (IB) courses in addition to limited numbers of AP (Advanced Placement) courses. Furthermore, the IB courses are offered at high level (HL) and standard level (SL). If a student is confident in his ability, he can enroll in HL. Otherwise, he can enroll in SL. When selecting high school classes, Lauda chose not only the IB Diploma pathway (see Chapter 4 for more details), but also all the available HL science classes including simultaneous enrollment in mathematics, physics and biology. This was not advisable, per his school counselor, as very few students had done this successfully. Many students who chose three HL science classes ended up quitting midway through and defaulting to SL. But Lauda was determined to challenge the counselor's wisdom, and he succeeded. With these most demanding and challenging courses, he was rewarded with a top GPA and the number one class rank when the time came for his college application. But, completing the courses was a tough period in his high school career. Lauda had to work hard. He formed study groups, and he associated with similar IB diploma students. The peer pressure to reach high achievements promoted high academic standing for each of his friends, too, who all ended up in top-tier colleges. The competition in the high school was friendly, but intense. We were hoping Lauda would be the valedictorian at his graduation ceremony, but we did not yet know.

Tip: A student should take as many high-level high school classes as he or she can achieve good grades in.

We had reason to be confident in our child. Lauda was quick to complete homework assignments, solve questions and then move on to the next task. He was well-organized; his bathroom and bedroom were tidy for a teenage boy. His handwriting, though, was like a stereotypical doctor's: It was hard to distinguish his "s" from his "f," his "b" from his "p," his "a" from his "d." June and I were concerned Lauda's writing score on the SAT I essay section would be miserably low, only because the scorer might not be able to read what Lauda wrote! (His real SAT score can be found in Chapter 3.) We told ourselves Lauda's brain worked so fast, his hands could not keep up with his thoughts.

By contrast, Lauda's younger brother Shaudi has nice, neat handwriting. Shaudi was slow, but thorough, in his homework. He would check references and make sure one thing was done well before moving on to the next. He also exchanged answers with friends via Facebook, IM (instant message), or cell phone texting. He checked formulas on Google. Shaudi usually studied alone at home, using social media to link with his study friends. These communication technologies were not widely used during Lauda's high school time. Often, Shaudi would get stuck on one piece of homework for the whole evening and did not have time to do his other class assignments. Shaudi also was less organized than Lauda. His bathroom, bedroom, and study area were messy. He lost many personal belongings, such as his cell phone, his iPod, and even articles of his clothing. Lauda never misplaced items.

When Shaudi was selecting high school courses at the same public high school Lauda had attended, we were conservative, based on what we knew about him, and did not encourage him to do the same three HL science subjects his brother did. Instead, Shaudi took 1 HL (chemistry) and then SL for the others (physics, math). The school counselor advised Shaudi against selecting more than one high level science class, just as the previous counselor had advised Lauda. Shaudi was happy he did not have to take more HL science subjects. But, he did follow his brother in accepting the challenge of the IB Diploma pathway. Shaudi managed a straight-A record from the 9th grade on, but he had a few A- grades. This brought down his GPA to a less-than-perfect 3.96. At Lauda's advice, Shaudi took the same Spanish classes his brother had, starting in the 7th grade and reaching Spanish 500 five years later. This helped Shaudi on the weighted class rank. He was 8th out of the graduating 579 students. But, Shaudi fell to 27th on the un-weighted scale. A student ranked 8th is much more likely to be accepted to a top-tier or Ivy-like college than a student ranked 27th, who would typically end up at a second-tier college. It shows the intensity of competition in high school: with Shaudi's straight-A record and GPA of 3.96, there were 26 students who performed academically stronger than he did.

So, assume that many students in a class take the same, tough subjects and perform equally well. How can one student stand out in the crowd?

Well, there are other strategies to increase class rank. In addition to taking all available HL subjects at his high school, Lauda also took an extra course online. There are many AP subjects offered online, sponsored by certified educational organizations, that may not be available at the local high school. One such website is *http://keystoneschoolonline.com/curriculum/advanced-courses*. A student can register, pay the fee, and start coursework at his own pace. If the student passes the final test, the score can be transferred to the high school transcript.

Another source for courses is the local community colleges where, typically, a student can take a more advanced course that is not available in the high school. Again, the score can be transferred to the high school transcript. This extra score will not change the GPA, but it can influence the weighted class rank.

Other websites provide instructions to help students to prepare for in-school AP courses and tests. These sites are for study assistance. They will not actually administer the test or transfer the scores. An example is: *http://www.montereyinstitute.org.*

Since high school coursework is already highly demanding, it can be difficult to earn these extra academic credits or commit time to extra preparation. It is better to achieve perfect grades from high school courses before taking any extra courses outside of the school. It is also important to check with the school counseling office to ensure these online and community college credits are accepted and counted for class ranking. These strategies would work particularly well for an intelligent student who attends a school with a limited offering of AP classes, thus preventing the student from spending free time on superfluous activities such as video games.

> *Tip: Check with the school counselor, but a high school student can usually take an extra course, online or through a community college, to increase class rank.*

In sports, it's the 0.01 seconds that makes world history in the Olympic Games. An old, Chinese saying states, "It is the one finishing stroke of brush to the eye that makes a painted dragon look alive." In academics, it's the 0.01 credits that set one student above the crowd, at the top of the class. For these tiny decimal numbers, a student must put in huge effort. But, hard work eventually pays the greater dividend.

Students, however, may prefer the video games.

Fulfilling both her parental roles – drill sergeant and champion – June was always on the lookout for our children to do extra work and fully use their time and energy. When Lauda was in 9th grade, school coursework did not burden him. He had considerable free time, so June signed him up for an online pre-calculus course, a pre-requisite for high school calculus.

Lauda resisted registering for the online course. He protested the extra work, even after June had paid the course fee. He did not log in to the course for a long time. When June checked his progress, only two weeks before course's expiration date, Lauda had not read a single word. June had done her champion role. Now, she became the drill sergeant, and enlisted my help.

I was in San Francisco for a meeting when June called. With me listening on the phone, June and Lauda had a heated exchange with high-pitched voices and sharp words. June was in tears and too emotional to compose rational arguments.

"I spent my whole life expending all my efforts on you since your birth and I sacrificed my medical career to raise you," she cried. "You do not even want to work to your potential. You hurt my heart."

Lauda shouted back: "You want me to study hard to get a better job so that I can pay you back? You want me to study for *you*! It is all for *you*!"

I was furious with Lauda's disrespect to June. I broke in and asked Lauda, "How do you think you should -- and can -- pay back your parents for caring for you?" I paused and listened to his silence. I then told him, "Go and get the work done."

At that time, June and I didn't have much leverage over Lauda. Curbing time spent on video games or out with friends did not work well. But, a disharmonious family session, or "tough love," while distasteful, did work. Lauda was "tough-loved" into action.

To our amazement, he completed the course in the two weeks remaining. We did not reward him for such good behavior, though, which was our mistake. Later, we learned that just as there are punishments for bad behavior, there also should be rewards for good. It is a fundamental principle in basic psychology called conditioning. Positive reinforcement produces positive behavior. Punishment may curb bad behavior, but it will not propagate good actions. When we took this lesson and applied it to Shaudi, it worked well.

There were many "tough love" sessions for both children growing up, described in later chapters, whether for academic "slackness" for a grade of A-, or for not practicing enough on their musical instruments. Our parental idea of punishment was like that described in *The Battle Hymn of The Tiger Mother*[2], although ours did not include physical punishment; cold, snowy temperature; or food deprivation. Yet, given the pressure from us, it is understandable we parents were sometimes the "enemy" to our children, especially during the rebellious teenage years. Shaudi had more than his share of the "tough love."

We worried both our children would grow up without feeling kindness from and toward us. At such moments, I always quoted an old adage to June: "All events, pleasant or poisonous, that passed, would become good memories in the future." We took comfort from this, and, indeed, typically an hour or so after the "tough love," while our facial muscles were still twisted, our children would forget the bad feeling and start to ask, "Mom, where's my calculator?" or "Dad, have you seen my math book?" (Of course the calculator was next to a stack of papers and the math book was on the dining room table, but both were somehow invisible to their teenage vision.) Whether that "short memory" was intentional, to ease family tension, or they had truly let it go and moved on, we did not know. We believed the latter. When asking Lauda today about hard feelings during "tough love" sessions, he could not recollect any particular events that had happened. Even Shaudi, who has more recently passed through the tough love stage, could not recall the bad feelings.

Indeed, in the later part of their high school careers, our voices did not need to be raised. Nor did we need a red face or a vein-engorged neck to make our points. It became much easier to take away the car keys or freeze our child's bank account. These "cool tools" achieved similar or better results than those produced during the earlier years' boiling emotions.

Detailing these unpleasant memories is important because June and I do believe most children need "tough love" to kick them into high gear, academically. If we leave them to their own feelings and wishes, most kids, although not all, will take the easy way, thus under-utilizing their capabilities. Many examples are in the following chapters.

Tip: Most children need parental "tough love" to kick them into high gear, academically.

There are debates regarding the impact of strict parenting on the development of a child's psychology, emotions, and self-esteem. Permissiveness is the central theme of child-rearing in Western culture, in distinct contrast to the view of Eastern culture, particularly Chinese culture, where ancient rules of child-rearing since the time of Confucius include: "strict teachers cultivate brilliant pupils" and "a tree will not grow tall and straight if not pruned, a person will not become great if not beaten up."

These days, even in China, parents do not follow the old teaching of "beating" a child to behave or restricting his activities, but parents in China are still stricter than those of us in the United States. As a result, children in Western cultures are more likely to be outgoing or extroverted. A child from an Eastern cultural environment is more likely to show humbleness and be a good listener or be introverted. It is debatable as to which personal traits are superior. But there is little argument that a child who is an academic high-achiever will move on to higher education, and higher education is an important factor for success in later life. We effectively raised our children using, predominantly, the "spice" of Eastern culture with some of the "sugar" of Western culture. Part of your parental responsibility is to figure out what ratio of sugar to spice will lead your child to academic success.

Chapter 3. SAT I and II scores (and the PSAT and ACT, too)

While GPA is an important factor in assessing a student's academic ability, it is far from the only measure colleges and universities value. As shown in the previous chapter, a GPA can be influenced by taking high-level, low-level or extra courses. It can also, of course, be the victim or beneficiary of teacher favoritism. So, many colleges and universities trust the Standardized Aptitude Test (SAT) to help capture the true strength of a student's academic performance.

The SAT represents the most objective measure of a student's academic strength. It is, therefore, among the standardized test scores requested directly after class rank and GPA on the academics section of the common application form. The SAT is a timed, closed-door test with proctors ensuring no cheating or assistance from unfair sources. The SAT is administrated by a private organization, the College Board, which has no direct relationship with any college. The test is available many times throughout the year, usually on Saturdays. Test dates and location can be found at www.collegeboard.org. The test typically takes place in a local high school. A student must register early to get into the test center closest to home. Having to journey to a test center farther from home can add to the student's stress, since it means he or she would have to get up even earlier on that Saturday morning.

> *Tip: A student should register early to take the SAT at the location closest to home.*

The SAT score is believed by some experts to be the "cutter," determining whether college or university admissions officers will spend more or less time on a student's application. For example, a student with a math score of 650 out of the full 800 math points possible may not be considered by a top-tier school of engineering.

Admissions officers need a way to manage the number of applications they must read, and the SAT helps these officers streamline their workload. Thus, it is obviously important to get as high an SAT score as possible.

The SAT I has three sections, plus an essay:

> English verbal/writing (up to 800 points)
> Critical reading (up to 800 points)
> Basic math (up to 800 points)
> Essay (up to 12 points)

The first three scores together total a maximum of 2400. The scores are reported separately in the college application form. This separation allows an admissions office to know the strength or weakness of a student in each academic area. The emphasis on English (two-thirds of the test) over math (one-third) places students with recent immigrant backgrounds at a disadvantage compared to those who speak English at home. Personally, I believe the weakness in science and engineering in the American schools and colleges is partly caused by the lesser demand on math from the SAT. The math section is relatively easy for most students with a science- or engineering-oriented family environment. This was certainly the case for our children.

3.1. The SAT I and PSAT

There are a flood of SAT I preparation books available in public libraries, bookstores, and online. A newer version or edition does not always mean a better book, as concepts commonly tested in a given subject typically remain similar, year after year. For example, there probably has not been a major discovery or advance in mathematics in half a century. But the format, or the way in which the concept is tested, may vary. Practice, practice, and practice is the only sure "trick" to ace the

27

tests. However, this is easier said than done. There were many battles over the years in our family for Lauda and Shaudi to practice for the SAT I.

Lauda was strong academically. Still, we started drilling him on SAT I vocabulary when he was in 7th grade. Because he had a non-English-speaking environment at home, we knew English was Lauda's weakest subject. We figured he would learn 10 new words a week, yielding 40 new words a month, or 480 new words a year. By his junior year, which was five years away, he would have learned 2,240 new words from this preparation, in addition to vocabulary from his regular school studies and from other sources. The plan was great, if we could stick to it. Using an SAT I vocabulary handbook, I wrote down ten new words in a notebook each week. I then drilled Lauda on the root meaning. He also had to use the word in a sentence. We practiced most evenings during the week and on weekends. Then, once a month, Lauda would summarize all the words he had learned in previous sessions. Lauda was cooperative and did very well. But as he advanced to high school, participated in sports teams, joined the music group and other clubs, and went out more frequently with friends for many excuses, his time spent at home became less and less. I would hardly see him when I was home from work. The plan failed to last very long. We did finish one small vocabulary book. We still have the notebook at home: ballpoint penned words diligently fill the first 40 pages. Those pages are wrinkled with wear. The remaining 60 pages are blank, untouched, a testament to our plan's disintegration. I don't know, but I do hope, the words from that little vocabulary book helped Lauda in his SAT I and school courses.

For Lauda's essay writing practice, once a month, I would clip the editorial essay at the end of a *Time* magazine. This would be his template. Using the same title, Lauda would write an essay, then compare his writing to the professional version. This allowed him to analyze his own essay's strengths and shortcomings. Lauda's writing was still his "weakest link," but I do feel his efforts and comparisons of his work to professional writings helped him understand his family's expectations and the importance of hard work.

Tip: Use a consistent home study method to work with your child to improve what you expect to be his or her weakest subject areas on the SAT I.

Later, Lauda attended a class for SAT enrichment organized at his high school, but he found it too easy. In the spring of his high school junior year, he finally took the test. He got scores that were decent, but less than perfect (math 780, critical reading 740, writing 720). June and I both believed Lauda could do better, at least in the math section. We wanted him to score a perfect 800. But Lauda believed his scores were good enough, and he refused to take the SAT I again. We discussed this with our private college counselor, who agreed with Lauda, so we gave our child his way. They were right, but we were assured only after Lauda was accepted into several Ivy League, New Ivy and Little Ivy colleges. If he had not been accepted into his "dream school," we would still be kicking ourselves for not pushing him hard enough to take the test again.

When Shaudi's time came to prepare for the SAT I, the situation was quite different. Shaudi matured slower. June had often considered letting Shaudi repeat a year in school. His birthday was in September, so more than two-thirds of the students in his class were older than he was. But Shaudi would not accept that idea. Further, the school would not allow it since his grades had been good, even though, emotionally, he was not up to his peers.

Contrary to the typical Asian belief of letting children start schooling early and advance quickly, many of our Western culture-minded friends were more concerned about their children's emotional and mental maturity at the early part of life and schooling. There are advantages to either concept. An older student in the class typically exhibits more confidence and is, naturally, more often placed in a leadership role. I, myself, had experienced both aspects of this concept. When I was in elementary school, I was the youngest in the class and followed bigger "brothers" around school activities or after-school play groups. In the 6th grade, I missed many months of school because of family issues. I had to repeat the grade. However, my role had flipped. I was now one of the oldest students in the class. Due to my seniority and strong academic performance, I was elected class president. I continued to serve as class president or student body officer at each grade for all subsequent years of my education, from grade school through college to graduate school. To this date, I am told I am the most confident, optimistic, and happy person in whatever I am doing. I am even "happy" to be an oncologist, working to help patients with the most difficult diagnoses.

With this in mind, June and I knew Shaudi, the baby of our family and a "baby" in his class, would need a lot of extra help early on if he were to get into an "Ivy League" caliber college. The school workload was light in the United States in comparison to other countries, especially China, where students in elementary school have to do homework until 10 p.m. We could add many extra classes for Shaudi outside of his regular school. As with Lauda, English was our greatest concern. Shaudi was enrolled in a Saturday afternoon English enrichment class with ten other Chinese children of similar age. With other mothers, June would usually sit in on the hourlong class. She would memorize the teacher's instructions for homework. The textbook was "Wordly Wise." It is available commercially at several levels of difficulty. We used this book at home for practice and thought it was a great textbook for home teaching or learning. There were vocabulary drills and sentence completion practice exercises using new words. Shaudi attended his English enrichment class for several years and performed well at his public school. We like to believe this extra help benefited his regular school grade.

While he was stronger in math, Shaudi did take some extra classes for enrichment in this subject as well. Initially, he attended a math class at the Chinese school for one hour on Saturday morning, after the morning Chinese lesson. Later, we hired a teacher to tutor him with another child of a family friend. Since there was no homework from the tutoring session, Shaudi didn't mind it. In 8th grade, when he took the Washington Assessment of Student Learning (WASL) test (which was replaced by High School Proficiency Exam, HSPE, in 2010), Shaudi's math was at the top tier level. When he took the SAT I test, his score qualified him to attend the summer programs at the University of Washington and Johns Hopkins University Center for Talent Youth (CTY). More information about the summer program can be found at *http://www.summer.washington.edu/summer/enroll/high_school.asp.* and *http://cty.jhu.edu/.*

Tip: Early enrichment classes can pay dividends years later.

Both Lauda at 7th grade and Shaudi at 8th grade took the SAT I before high school. There are some major benefits to this. SAT I scores taken before 9th grade are not transmitted to colleges; any SAT score taken after entering 9th grade will be reported to any college a student later applies to for admission. Therefore, any attempt at the SAT I after the 9th grade should be a serious one. Taking the test earlier (for timing refer to table in Chapter 1.2) not only helped both Lauda and Shaudi get into summer enrichment programs, but it also prepared their and June's and my minds about the formality of the test and the expectations we should have of it.

Tip: For special benefits, and to best prepare for the real exam, a student should take a practice SAT I test before high school.

As Shaudi progressed in school, gained his own ideas, and dealt with increasing demands of school-related homework, it became increasingly difficult for June and me to convince him to do any "extra" lessons. We loosened up on him until he was in 10th grade. That's when we received the results from his PSAT. The PSAT, or pre-SAT, is a high-stakes practice for the real SAT I test. A PSAT score that reaches the 95th percentile qualifies a student as a National Merit Semi-finalist. The student must submit a short essay to compete to be a National Merit Scholar finalist. Many colleges recognize this merit, and offer scholarships to these students. A finalist medal significantly enhances any student's college application. The score itself is not reported in the application form, but the honor is listed on the form as described in Chapter 5. Again, there are many preparation books for the PSAT. We neglected this preparation and practice when Shaudi wanted more time for life and less time for study.

Shaudi's PSAT score was disappointing to him and seriously concerned us. He did not even meet the level for National Merit Scholar semi-finalist selection. His English section was the most in need of improvement. We talked with him about the test results and analyzed areas of weakness and strength. Shaudi accepted that he needed to get back to extra lessons and effort, and was less rebellious to our suggestions. We scratched our heads and asked friends for their experience in using private English tutoring.

To our surprise, there were many private tutoring services. Some were professional, full-time, private tutors who travelled from one student's home to the next or who hosted students in their own homes during the afternoon, after school hours, or on weekends. Some tutors were high school seniors, while others were employed by private organizations which hire or contract tutors for a group of students. The tutors all charged an hourly rate, which was highly variable depending on the experience of the tutor. We saw rates ranging from $20 to $100. To find a tutor, we used sources including word of mouth, local library postings, local newspaper ads, and a Google search. We performed screening and interviewing, and hired a tutor who was also recommended by a friend who had used the tutor for her daughter. Shaudi started one-on-one lessons on Saturday afternoons in the local library. On the first day of each month, we would call the library to book a study room for a set time every Saturday in that month. There were many similar tutoring activities going on, so the study rooms were a highly sought-after commodity. I sat in for Shaudi's first few sessions. The tutor used SAT I preparation books and tests to lead the study, and analyzed the result when Shaudi did not get the correct answer. The most challenging part for Shaudi was long critical reading and comprehension passages. There was minimal homework from the tutor after the sessions. These classes continued for about a semester. Over time, however, we detected that Shaudi felt this one-on-one setting was becoming rather boring. Worse, when we tested him at home, we did not see any improvement.

To improve the study environment and to share the cost, we found another friend whose daughter was at the same grade level as Shaudi and also in need of extra help in English. The semi-private tutoring went on for another term. We tested Shaudi again at home using three sets of SAT I questions to determine an average score. To June's and my disappointment, there was still no improvement in his critical reading. We were in despair. We kept all the previous tests and his answer sheets, and compared notes. Shaudi was convinced he needed to change his strategy. So, during the school break for the summer, we started to search again for a private tutoring school, rather than private tutors.

We decided to move to a tutoring school instead of a private tutor because we believed the school would have screened teachers for their qualifications, and, presumably, have a curriculum. It is hard for parents to find a good tutor to suit the child's learning style, so a school might have more personnel options. Finally, we found a private education service in our area that fit our purpose. Friends' children who attended the school provided some of their thoughts and recommendations. We met with the principal, who owned the service. He interviewed us and Shaudi together, then separately. We expressed our concern about Shaudi's critical reading difficulties and our desire for him to improve. This private education service also offered enrichment in courses such as math, chemistry, physics, etc. There was also a real-time, simulated SAT I test. There were specially designed, curricula, assigned *New York Times* or *Washington Post* articles for reading, and general scientific papers to browse. There were five to six students in one class for a two-hour session each Saturday. We signed for Shaudi to join the program.

We received progress reports from the enrichment school and we would also check Shaudi's binder to evaluate his progress. There was, at last, some improvement in his critical reading skills. Not surprisingly, there were many students, mostly Asian, taking these Saturday classes. We liked this setting of private tutoring much better than our previous experiences. We would recommend a similar service to fellow parents seeking private tutoring for a student who still has additional free time, particularly in the 8th, 9th, or early 10th grade, before taking the real college entrance SAT I.

Tip: If parents feel they cannot help a student improve in a subject area, consider hiring a private tutor, but ensure the student still makes progress.

It would soon be time for Shaudi to take the SAT I at the high school level. We felt he needed still another format of tutoring. Ideally, a student should ace the SAT I on the first attempt. Although students are allowed to take the SAT I as many times as they want, there is the perilous possibility of getting lower scores in subsequent attempts. Colleges do allow students to pick their highest scores on the various SAT I sections from different testing sessions and to report the combined highest total score. But colleges and universities do receive all test scores once the student is in the 9th grade. Thus, a college or university knows how many attempts a student has made. A declining score will be a red flag for top-tier college admissions officers. Furthermore, a combined highest score of, for example, 2,200, from a student with multiple attempts would be less impressive than that same score from a student who took the test just once. Rejecting students with perfect scores of 2,400 was once fashionable at top-tier colleges. It created a sense of competitiveness and attractiveness. But, I bet those rejected "perfect" scorers were those with a combined 2,400 from multiple SAT I attempts.

> *Tip: To be most impressive to colleges, a student should ace the SAT I on the first attempt.*

There is a test called the TOEFL (Test of English as a Foreign Language) that attempts to evaluate English language proficiency for non-native speakers. Foreign college graduates who have to take the TOEFL test and score well know the tricks of getting a high score. They also know a high score does not always mean better language skills when it comes to working in an English speaking country. There is an important element of skill in test-taking. That skill can be derived from the same mantra of former U.S. Republican Party Vice-Presidential Candidate Sarah Palin: "Drill, baby, drill!"

Based on this philosophy, we looked for SAT I crash courses. In these courses, students practice simulated tests over and over again. We did find several services that met our criteria. These were nationwide education companies, but we cannot provide names due to commercial conflicts. Typically, such services offer a short-term SAT preparation course lasting 8-10 weeks. Each session lasts 2-3 hours over the weekend. There can be many students (10 or more), depending on the season and time of the year. The tutors are typically well-screened by the company, and many of them have to take the SAT regularly and receive a high score to be qualified as instructors. They also receive training in instructional skills. We believe the investment in taking one or more of these courses is worthwhile. When we signed Shaudi up, it was low season for student attendance. There was a sales promotion with a 30% fee discount. Shaudi had intensive, in-class sessions for two hours every Saturday. There were no homework assignments other than more practice tests at home. In essence, it was practice, practice, practice; or drill, drill, drill.

Ideally, a student should take the real SAT I two to three weeks after completing the preparation course in order to absorb the new material yet not to forget testing skills learned in the class. This approach worked well for Shaudi. His final score for his first SAT I attempt was 2,240 (math 800, writing 730, critical reading 710). As predicted, critical reading was still Shaudi's downfall. But these scores were competitive enough for Ivy League level colleges. We discussed with him the possibility of a second attempt. Shaudi complained: "Why do I have to do all these extra studies while my friends and classmates aren't? They're having more fun and they have a good life." Knowing his strength and weakness, we compromised. After all, Shaudi could not do any better in the math section. He might improve his score in the writing section, but the reading score was already the highest we had ever seen from him. There was a real chance that reading score could go lower on subsequent attempts. Shaudi got his way and we kept our promise to buy him a guitar, the reward for his high score.

This reward was not an accident. The guitar was part of our SAT I strategy.

During Lauda and in Shaudi's early years, June and I had hated the confrontational exchanges when we "tough-loved" them to do extra work. In preparing for the SAT I, though, we had calculated that if Shaudi could score at least a 2,200 (which meant above the 90th percentile; 2,200÷2,400=91.7%), he would be a "grade A" student among the high school students across the country who took the test at the same time. That would be a commendable academic status. So, we employed our strategy. One week before Shaudi started the SAT I crash course, June and I asked him, "What is your wish if you could get anything you want?"

Shaudi replied, "I would like a guitar to teach myself how to play."

He did not know we were throwing out "bait," and he certainly did not have any reason to suspect or put up defenses against our "secret" SAT I calculation.

"Okay," we countered, "We will buy you a guitar if you can get over 2,200 on your first SAT I attempt."

Periodically, we jokingly reminded him about our deal, noting, "You are really working hard for your new guitar," when we saw him study. He did not complain about the extra work on Saturdays while his friends were having fun. When his final SAT I score was in, he was so excited.

"I want to buy the guitar right now!" he said.

We were pleased, but a bit anxious Shaudi would choose a guitar that was unreasonably expensive. Furthermore, since this would be his first guitar, what if he tried it and did not like it? June reacted quickly, showing only our pleasure, not our concern.

"Yes!" she said. "You earned it. Let me help you shop for it."

June directed Shaudi to the website for the Costco warehouse store. She knew this would be cheaper than a guitar at a professional music store. To our relief, Shaudi ordered a guitar that cost less than $200. He has been playing it ever since, learning notes from friends and online tips.

Tip: If a student isn't sufficiently motivated, try offering an affordable incentive to reward a test score that reaches a certain number.

Due to the content and intensity of the SAT I crash courses, we would not recommend this method for a student who is still a long time away from taking the real SAT I. Several students of our close family friends followed Shaudi's track and achieved similarly desirable test results. But, parents need to be encouraging, not threatening. With the lesson learned from Shaudi's SAT I guitar, we finally believed in the tried and true statement: "The drive from within is a lot more powerful and desirable than that applied from outside" We did work with Lauda to prepare him for the SAT I, but he did not need the intense work Shaudi required. Had we left Shaudi to do things his own way, he would have taken the easier path and not had a chance to attend an Ivy-level college. June and I felt fulfilled by the efforts we exerted on behalf of both of our very different children.

3.2. The SAT II

The SAT II is also known as the subject test. The test may examine any subject taught at the high school level such as chemistry, physics, biology, world history, American history, a foreign language (Spanish, French, Chinese, etc.), math levels, and so forth. Some people believe the subject test captures a student's true academic strength and plays an essential role in admissions evaluation. After all, when a college admits a student, it truly wants the student to succeed. If the student cannot keep up with his or her class in college or, worse, quits the college due to academic difficulties, the admissions officer's judgment is called into question.

The SAT II is also particularly important for high-achieving high school students. This is because it is conceivable that a college or university has an SAT I threshold for acceptance, for example, 2,160 (hypothetically). This would mean an SAT I score of 2,400 would be no more impressive to that top-tier college than 2,160. In this case, it would be SAT II scores and other aspects of the application that would determine whether or not the student is accepted.

So, we did not lighten our pressure on Lauda and Shaudi after their good, but not perfect, SAT I scores. June bought many SAT II preparation books, both new and used. The SAT I and II books at our home were stacked three feet tall at one point. Lauda liked to study by himself with these prep books, and he went through many of them. Most of the top-tier colleges require two SAT subject tests, while a few colleges do not ask for a SAT II test at all. Among the top-tier colleges, only Harvard College requires three SAT II tests. Early in his senior year of high school, Lauda took both the math level IIC test and the physics test in one Saturday morning. He took a biology test the next Saturday morning. He did well on them: math was a perfect score of 800, physics was 780, biology was 760.

As usual, when it was his turn, Shaudi needed more hand-holding, championing, and "tough-loving." He wanted to take only two subject tests.

"It's too hard to do three," he reasoned.

"So, which two subject tests do you want to take?" June probed.

"Chemistry and math," Shaudi answered.

"Considering that you'll take the IB chemistry test soon in school, it might be a good idea to take SAT II chemistry first since the preparation would benefit both," June advised.

Chemistry was more interesting to Shaudi than physics. His school grade was A, so we thought he could do well on that SAT II area.

Shaudi began self-study at home using the books Lauda had used. However, Shaudi soon realized not all contents of the SAT chemistry test were covered by his high school chemistry class. He was disconcerted by his simulated test score. June looked into tutoring, again, with the same company Shaudi used to study for his SAT I crash course. She reported we could choose from two different tutors. Having learned from having our time and money wasted with the one-on-one private tutoring, I prepared a list of questions and interviewed each tutor over the phone. Our conversations were similar:

Q. What teaching material do you use? Do you use the same book repetitively or change books frequently?
A. I use a standardized study manual provided by the company; it's one book.

Q. During the session, how do you conduct tutoring, i.e., going over concepts versus testing?
A. At the first session, I give a diagnostic test to identify 10 weak areas. I then clarify the concepts and give a practice test.

Q. How often do you administer practice tests?
A. There are at least two simulated tests.

Q. How many students are you tutoring now? How many have you tutored in the past year? What were their scores?
A. I am working with two other students now and had tutored many in the past. I do not know the scores, as the students didn't report back.

Q. Would you provide names of former students for reference?
A. Yes. But they are at college now and may not respond to you.

Q. Do you prepare for each student and session differently, or do you use the same protocol for all students?

A. I prepare for each student and session differently and I do not use the same protocol for all students.

Q. Do you have to be certified as a tutor by the company that employs you?
A. Definitely

Q. What personal advice would you give a student to ace the test?
A. Practice, practice, and practice!

Both tutors were college students. They each answered the questions nicely and confidently. Both were certified by the company to tutor several subjects. But then, upon more probing, their biographies and their answers to new questions diverged. One was in his third year of college, majoring in chemistry at our local university. The other was tutoring full-time, taking a year off from his out-of-town college to return home to earn more money for his future tuition. When I asked the tutor who attended our local university how he juggled his own study with tutoring, he gave a thoughtful answer about his scheduling. When I asked the tutor who was taking a year off from his studies how he juggled his own study with tutoring, he said it wasn't a problem. The tutor, who was also studying, of course, had less time available to tutor. The tutor who was taking time off from school had more availability.

Honestly, June and I weren't sure if the tutor who was taking time off from school really was stopping his own studies so he could better fund them. But, we gave him the benefit of the doubt and the opportunity to earn his "tuition." I called the director of the enrichment school with our decision. Soon, Shaudi received the background knowledge tests for both chemistry and math level IIC. He completed them and returned the answer sheets. As we anticipated, Shaudi's chemistry would need extra help but his math did not. We figured out the date of his SAT II chemistry test and started our parental chauffeuring duty to the enrichment school seven

41

weeks prior to the test date. The tutoring was for a total of ten hours in five sessions over five Saturdays. Shaudi would also have two extra weekends to refresh and clarify any concepts he still struggled to understand. Shaudi did well above our expectations on both subjects as shown in Chapter 11 under the sample student JJB profile.

We also had an unusual dilemma regarding Shaudi's SAT II biology test. Though he did not ask to take it, he was required to according to a contract we had signed with the Seattle BioQuest Institute for a summer behavioral research project. But, Shaudi did not take a biology class in high school. We feared he would have a disastrous score and this would hurt his college admission. I called the research project supervisor and explained our concern. She assured us that since Shaudi would be taking the SAT II biology test for a research project, the score could be withheld from colleges. All we had to do was inform the College Board of our situation and ask it not to release the score if it was not ideal. The summer behavioral research project had been running for several years at the BioQuest Institute, so the research project supervisor was used to such parental concerns. Her project was funded by a National Institutes of Health grant to study participating students' college science performance and future career choices, given their early exposure to real-life science. Participants had to take the SAT II biology test and complete surveys when entering college and two years later. The SAT II biology scores would be compared to the national average. In return, participants had opportunities to shadow BioQuest scientists who were working on real-life biological research, such as finding vaccines for HIV or Malaria. Students were also compensated for their time and expenses for meals and transportation. It was a great experience for Shaudi, and these feelings were reflected in one of his college short essays, as listed in Chapter 7.

But, we did not yet know how this real-world experience would translate into test-taking. In preparation for the SAT II biology exam, June bought yet another practice book. Shaudi spent two weekends reviewing it, all by himself. We selected the last test date available, in December, to allow him more time to prepare. We were astonished two weeks later when his test score was released. When June called me at work, I asked many times, "It's 750? Are you sure? Go back and check it again." June re-checked with Shaudi on the College Board website. "Shaudi is no longer our 'baby,'" I declared. "He has matured and possesses talent leading to success, if he devotes himself. Shaudi has earned our respect."

There were no more "tough-love" sessions. In fact, Shaudi had wanted an iPod Touch, but we had resisted because of his penchant to lose personal belongings, such as a cell phone and an iPod Mini. But, after seeing his impressive SAT II biology score, we granted him permission to buy the device.

Was this high score the luck of pure chance? Or was it the result of the summer bio-research job shadowing experience? Neither option could fully explain Shaudi's success. Giving random responses, or even blindfolded, a student might expect to get 25% of the answers correct. If the student was really lucky on the sunny test day, 50% correct answers would be the maximum expectation for pure luck. To get more than 90% of the answers correct, Shaudi proved he truly knew the subject. In trying to trace his success, June and I broadened our thinking. The summer job shadowing did have seminars, in addition to observing experiments conducted by the scientists. But the teaching was mainly at a philosophical level to explain how science could change the lives of human beings and treat fatal diseases. There were no basic biology concepts or actual experimental protocols taught. We also knew Shaudi had studied the SAT II biology book June had purchased for him. But that was two weekends of work, hardly enough for such a stellar score. We searched our minds and reflected upon summer enrichment camps, the summer program at the University of Washington and Johns Hopkins Talented Youth camp, and so many other academic programs Shaudi experienced. Finally, we concluded, Shaudi's SAT II biology success probably stemmed from a combination of many educational activities he did over the years. Sometimes, general sustained effort leads to specific success in unexpected areas.

> *Tip: Books are important, but experience can also form a quality education.*

3.3. The ACT

The ACT is administrated by ACT, an organization in competition with the SAT administrator, the College Board. Both organizations are not-for-profit, and both promote the strength or accuracy of their test to reflect a student's academic capability. Consequently, there are marketing campaigns from each organizer. For example, ACT explains its test is an achievement test, measuring what a student has learned in school. ACT describes the SAT I, therefore, as more of an aptitude test, testing reasoning and verbal abilities. The College Board, meanwhile, bills the SAT I as a globally recognized college admission test and states the combination of high school grades and SAT scores is the best predictor of academic success in college.

The truth is, either one is fine for most college or university applications. However, there are some geographic prejudices about the two tests across the United States. More students from the coastal states take the SAT, while more students in the central states take the ACT. This SAT/ACT map almost resembles the distribution of blue states and red states in the presidential elections.

The composition of the tests also varies. The ACT has math, reading, English, and science, as well as an optional essay. The SAT I does not have science. The maximum ACT score is 32 for each area. The small essay added to the SAT I in 2005 is not reported separately in the application form. Some students who outperform their peers on the SAT I do more poorly on the ACT, and vice-versa.

In trying to decide which exam is better for a specific child, it may be worthwhile to have the child complete a simulation test for each test. Again, many preparation books are available at public libraries and bookstores for the ACT. There are also, of course, private tutoring services.

> Tip: If trying to choose between the SAT I and ACT, let a
> student take a simulation of each exam to determine
> which score starts out higher.

The ACT does seem to be gaining popularity. In our local public school district, for example, 333 students out of a total of 1,720 students took the ACT in 2010. That same year, 880 students took the SAT I. (The remaining 30% of high school seniors did not take either and probably were not considering a four-year college.) Though the number of students taking the ACT was a fraction of the number of students taking the SAT I, the number of students taking the ACT was up 30% from 2008 (*www.nsd.org*).

A policy that could push students toward the ACT or repel them from the ACT is score reporting. A student can request the ACT send a college admissions office only the student's best ACT score, regardless of how many ACT attempts the student made. Meanwhile, if a student asks the College Board to send SAT results, it will release a full SAT test history. However, the College Board allows a mishmash, highlighting the highest SAT score from different tested areas on different test dates, to report a combined highest total score. The ACT does not allow such cherry picking.

Many college admissions officers told us they did not have a preference for one test over the other.

Chapter 4. AP and IB Scores and Current Courses

The sections for test scores and current courses are next to each other on the Common Application Form. The AP (Advanced Placement) and IB (International Baccalaureate) scores provide further objective data for admissions officers to assess a student's academic strength. This is because these tests and scores are not subject to an individual school's variation or teacher bias. AP exams are developed and scored by the College Board, the same New York City-based organization that administers and scores the SAT. IB curriculum is directed by the International Baccalaureate organization, headquartered in Geneva, Switzerland.

AP is more popular and is available in more high schools than IB. AP is also easier for a school to organize. For example, in the entire state of Washington, with a total of 436 high schools, only 16 high schools are approved to offer IB courses. By contrast, more than 300 Washington high schools offer AP courses. There are also many online AP courses that may offer extra credits beyond a local high school can offer.

However, an IB score is more recognized and accepted internationally, while an AP score is less well comprehended by colleges outside of America. Further information on comparisons of the two programs can be found at _www.ibo.org_ and _www.ibo.org/ibna/documents/ibandap.pdf_.

The option to take an AP or IB course may depend on the high school the student attends. Some high schools offer either an AP or an IB course; some offer both. To get into a top-tier university, a student should try as many AP or IB courses as he or she can handle. Taking these high-level courses offers a number of advantages in the college application process:

Many colleges and universities will not only accept these courses, they will, if the student passes with a high enough score, waive the subject in college. This can mean a considerable savings in tuition.

Due to their high level of difficulty, these courses can also bring up a student's weighted GPA and class rank, as mentioned in Chapter 2.

A student loaded with successful AP or IB courses is more like to impress an admissions officer as a hardworking, driven, challenge-seeking individual. These are personal traits sought by top tier colleges. After all, college is about education and learning.

In the IB program there are two options: the IB Certificate and the IB Diploma. The certificate can work like AP courses: A student takes a subject, passes the test, and gets college credits if the test score is high enough. Individual colleges and universities decide what score they will accept. To earn an IB Diploma, however, a student must pass end-of-course exams in each of the six, core IB classes with a minimum score of 4 out of 7. The student must also write a 4,000-word research essay, called TOK (Theory of Knowledge), and write a 1,500-word regular essay. IB test papers are scored by specially trained IB teachers around the world. In 2008, only 339 students in the entire state of Washington earned an IB Diploma. At our local high school, 87 students graduated with IB Diplomas in the 2009-2010 class of 570.

The benefits of a student loading up on IB courses are the same if not more than for a student loading up with AP courses. Some states even give IB special recognition. On Feb. 25, 2011, for example, the Washington State House

Committee on Education voted 19-2 to approve a law recognizing that students who complete the IB Diploma satisfy the requirements for high school graduation.

Students can take IB courses without taking the exam, which is similar to a student taking an AP course but not the AP exam. For example, in our local school district of three high schools, the 2009-2010 school year saw 749 students enrolled in AP courses. Of these, 1,166 exams were taken with a 69% pass rate. This statistic indicates some students took more than one course and exam, while some took the courses but not the exams.

Both Lauda and Shaudi took the IB Diploma pathway and passed their exams with high scores. It was, indeed, very challenging work. Frequently, they worked late into the night and used most of the weekends for study as well. But, in the end, the results were rewarding to them, and to June and me as parents, too. An unexpected benefit was that they associated with other IB Diploma students. Their friends were all high academic achievers. They worked together, called on each other frequently, and went to parties together. The positive peer pressure was in sharp contrast to the commonly heard peer pressure of alcohol or drug abuse in high school, or friends who spent their time on the more typical, mundane interests of teenagers like brand name shoes and fancy clothing. Lauda and Shaudi truly did not have time to do anything "bad." The program effectively acts like a "high school Ivy League," bringing the smartest minds together. Students taking individual IB or AP course would not have this extra benefit of this group association.

Tip: Academically inclined peers can help keep a high school student on track, especially if they take challenging classes together.

Not to say we left our sons to make all their decisions by virtue of positive associations. We participated in our sons' course selections. A selection of difficult courses shows a student's determination to challenge his potential, while a more

49

relaxed course selection tells the tale of a student wanting to get into a college, but lacking inner drive. As mentioned previously, Lauda selected more high level (HL) courses. We did not encourage Shaudi to do as many; rather, we suggested he do some HL and more standard level courses. The HL courses did help to push Lauda's class rank to the top, while Shaudi's class rank suffered. However, parents must remain attuned to a child's unique abilities.

Chapter 5. Honors and Awards

Honors and awards are the icing on the cake, the medals of decoration. They surely help a student shine in the large crowd of college and university applicants. These awards can come from any source: academic, sports, social activities, arts, or volunteer work. Whatever the honor or award, it provides a mark of recognition and distinction for the student. Earning distinction is a worthwhile endeavor for a student to consciously pursue. But these honors and awards are typically given by others, and cannot be requested. A student needs to work hard for them, and wisely strategize his or her use of energy and time.

There are many national, regional and local opportunities for honors and awards. Most students are not aware of many outside opportunities that can add to their achievements. As Elizabeth Wissner-Gross stated in her book, *What Colleges Don't Tell You (And Other Parents Don't Want You to Know)*[3], the most successful students have a parent or mentor constantly on the lookout for new contests, internships, paid jobs, and the like. A few years ago, the daughter of one of our friends submitted a paper to the *SiemensWestinghouse* Competition (*www.siemens-foundation.org/en/competition.htm*) and won the top prize. Her paper was generated from her summer research at a university medical center where her father, our friend, worked. Due to her father's connections, she was able to work under a different investigator every summer since the 8th grade. The continuity helped her to complete her winning project. The prize also was a key factor in her being accepted to the top-tier colleges to which she applied. She had a hard time deciding which one to attend.

A son of another friend of ours had been keenly interested in automation and robotic toys since childhood. His science courses and grades in high school were good, but his humanities classes and grades were distressing to his parents. He was on the school's Science Olympiad Team for several consecutive years and participated in a number of competitions, locally and regionally. But, the team never won a top prize. The student later submitted his own work to the Intel Science Talent Search (*www.intel.com/about/corporateresponsibility/education*). Finally, he won a prize. It was not the top prize, but it did benefit him greatly, not only financially, but also in gaining him acceptance to several top engineering colleges.

As evidenced by these examples, national-level prizes carry much greater weight for a college applicant than simply the illustriousness of the honor itself. These prizes can be keys to college doors.

Luckily, there are many options.

If a student is really good at math, there is the international Olympic Math Competition. A student can sign up and try to win the medal, which can pave an impressive path to a top-tier engineering college.

Similarly good credentials for a music student could be serving as first chair for violin in a regional orchestra.

An athletically-inclined child could topple the competition in sports contests.

In *Battle Hymn of the Tiger Mother* by Amy Chue, the elder daughter's achievement in piano was impressive, with performances given at Carnegie Hall and other national forums. By this talent alone, she would be in an extremely competitive position for any top-tier college of university. With her decent academic grades (pushed by her mother), she would be a "hot asset" to be grabbed by every top-tier admissions officer. In terms of extreme athletic ability, there are many stories about Olympic medalists who, after retiring from sports, earned acceptance into top-notch colleges.

All these national and international awards and honors do not come easily, however. Students must dedicate a tremendous amount of hard work, determination, and time. Parents must give their own effort, guidance, willingness and have the ability to pay fees. Parents also must constantly be on the lookout for opportunities. Public school guidance counselors, and even private school guidance counselors, are not often equipped to find these niche activities due to their workload.

Tip: Parents should help students learn about and enter competitions, since honors and awards can garner positive attention from college admissions officers.

Most students can achieve more realistic awards or honors from regional or local competitions. Since Lauda and Shaudi attended the same public school, their awards and honors were quite similar. Both were on the school Science Olympiad team. Lauda's team won several regional awards while Shaudi's won some local ones. Both held honors from the National Honor Society. Both were high school varsity tennis team captains. Their teams won district-wide championships. Both played classical musical instruments, but were not sufficiently proficient to garner any awards or honors. We were on the lookout for bigger opportunities, but the outcomes were not always as grandiose as we had wished. For example, Lauda conducted research in the summer and after school at the Fred Hutchinson Cancer Research Center, similar to the facility where the daughter of our friend generated her research that, as mentioned above, won her the top prize in the *Siemens* Westinghouse Competition. Lauda learned about and observed a number of laboratory techniques and concepts. But, he did not have an independent project, which could have led to publication or a competition submission. People who do laboratory research and hang their lives on the "publish or perish" refrain appreciate the degree of luck in research. Some scientists struggle for years without a publication, while others are highly prolific within a short time. Lauda did not achieve what June and I had hoped, but his research experience did have a positive influence on his college application: one college offered him paid summer research jobs and a five-year track to a master's degree. He did not accept this offer, but it was nice to receive it. Shaudi, meanwhile, did not do bench research. He tried clinical research, instead. Shaudi collected and arranged data from patient chart reviews. He did not have enough knowledge to write a paper, since comprehending the clinical significance of the information would require the expertise of an experienced physician. Shaudi did manage, however, to get a co-authorship in the final publication that he listed in his Common Application Form.

How much local or regional awards or honors help a student's application is not known. They are nice to have, but unlikely to be the determining factor for college admission. Nevertheless, the effort and process are good practice in hard work.

Tip: Even if an attempt doesn't lead to an award or honor, help your child find value in lessons learned, and possibly apply those lessons elsewhere on the college application.

Chapter 6. Extracurricular Activities

Generally, a well-rounded student is more desirable to a college or university than one with narrow or unusual interests. There also is value to a student who can bring a different perspective due to uncommon factors in his or her background, education, activities, or culture. Many colleges take particular interest in looking for such students, since these students can add to classroom and campus diversity. A "bookworm" who studies but does not participate in any other activities may achieve higher grades and academic standing in high school, but may not be a strong college applicant for a variety of other reasons.

As parents, we probably all hear stories about high school students who eat lunch alone and move around the campus without friends. From our experience as adults, we know it is important for a person's well-being to interact with others. Most of us thrive in a community. "Loners" may not fit into the essential social fabric of a long-range career. More alarmingly, incidents of campus shooting more often are perpetrated by loners than by more social students.

Tip: Don't let a student study so much that he or she doesn't have time to cultivate friends or outside interests.

Extracurricular activities build a sense of community, teamwork, and society. Outside activities are beneficial to a child's well-being. They also happen to help when it comes time for college admissions.

Remember: Spare time and energy are precious for a student, especially during the later years of high school. So, the student should allocate his or her time wisely.

There are many non-academic activities to get involved in, both at school and outside of school. But, for enhancing university application credentials, it is not the numbers of activities that matter. Instead, it is the depth of involvement that makes the difference.

6.1. Sports

Both Lauda and Shaudi played sports when they were growing up. Lauda played soccer on the community team when he was in elementary school. We watched him with mixed feelings. We initially thought that, with his short stature and fine coordination, he could be a fast runner and, hopefully, a good soccer player. But, instead of running after the ball, Lauda always waited for the ball to come to him. His team quickly lost. Lauda then tried swimming. However, he was water-phobic until 4th grade, and both arms had been fractured earlier due to overextension. He could not make it onto a swim team, much less achieve any awards in this field. Lauda was not interested in baseball, and we never thought he would be good at football due to his size and weight. Finally, he settled on tennis and found it fun. Lauda started to play tennis in middle school in preparation for getting onto the high school team. Tennis is a "cut" sport in high school, meaning a team can only accept a limited numbers of players. So, a student must be good to get on the team. Having an early start and continued practice is essential.

Luckily, there often are many community facilities for tennis, since it is a popular sport for adults, too. Private, semi-private, or group lessons are easily available. When he first started playing, Lauda signed up for group lessons at our local community tennis club. Later, he played at several tennis clubs in our area. Coaches from the club would take the team to US Tennis Association (USTA) age group tournaments around the region. If a player wishes, he or she can also sign up for a USTA competition by age group. Schedules and locations are posted on the USTA website at *www.USTA.com*. After school and on weekends, June would chauffeur Lauda to wherever his tennis interest led the car. Her odometer reading suffered, but Lauda did not. He made the cut to play on his school's junior varsity team when he entered 9th grade. Later, he made it to the varsity team. In his senior year, he became the team captain. Though June no longer had to drive long distances, Lauda still had to allocate quite a bit of time to afterschool practices and competitions, particularly during the fall season (August to November for the boys' team; girls' tennis is a spring season sport). Lauda would go to a practice or competition after school at around 2:30 p.m., not arriving home until around 6-7 p.m. every day during the season. He had to stay up late to finish his homework. His team did win some local and regional titles. Later, Lauda's college application form proudly displayed the time spent on tennis and the awards won from it.

Having tested different sports for Lauda, it was easier to narrow down which sports would best suit Shaudi. When he was little, Shaudi would follow his older brother around, admiringly. Once, when a doctor prescribed Lauda an inhaler for his persistent cough and possible asthma, Shaudi protested that we must buy him an inhaler, too. So, Shaudi quickly settled on tennis, and June and I went through the identical steps and routes -- in fact the same tennis clubs and sometimes the same coach -- as we had with Lauda. As high school neared, Shaudi, who had been short and chubby as a child, was taller and had a longer arm span than his brother's. His footwork was slower, but his serve was more powerful. Shaudi made it to the high school junior varsity and later to the varsity tennis team. He also played in USTA tournaments with a club team, so Shaudi won some local titles both for the school and for himself.

The members of the high school team elected their captain. We had encouraged both our sons to take a leadership role. When the coach called out, "Would the players who are interested in being our team captain step out please?" several candidates did. The one who received the most votes became the captain, typically the most senior player. Lauda had the most votes and became the captain, while Shaudi tied with another player and became a co-captain. Both were assets to their teams, as was June, who would follow the team to competitions to bring food and drinks.

We were fortunate that our sons found their athletic passions rather early. There are so many possibilities for sports activities. Once a child shows interest in a particular sport, it is important for parents to help keep the child motivated. It is also more fun if the school has a team for that sport. After all, most children want to have fun, yet, if a child really excels in a sport, it is a significant asset for a college application.

Recently, we attended an open house for newly admitted students to a top-tier college. During the self-introductions, we learned four students from the same high school had earned admission to that college. These students were all on the same swimming relay team that won the regional high school swimming relay championship. Similarly, two girls from Lauda and Shaudi's high school were admitted to Stanford University. We later found out the two girls were synchronized water dance partners and had won some awards.

Whatever sport a child ends up enjoying, winning awards and a championship can be keys to top college doors. If the parent is worried the child may not excel in enough other areas for the admissions officer to grant entry, the sport's coach at the desired college can be the biggest ally for the applicant. Contacting the coach early during the application process can enhance the child's chance of successful entry to a highly selective college.

6.2. Arts

While sports and other physical activities challenge the body and promote coordination of the arms and legs, music stimulates the mind. Playing instruments can promote brain and fine motor control and coordination. Although neither June nor I had the resources or opportunities to learn any musical instruments when we were growing up, we wanted our children to have a chance to learn an instrument. Both Lauda and Shaudi started piano lessons when they were in preschool. After a few years of learning the piano and understanding the basics of music, Lauda wanted to try to play the violin. However, unlike the piano, as Lauda got larger, the size of his violin would also need to increase. Because instruments can be expensive, music teachers recommended we rent instruments as Lauda grew, then buy him a properly sized violin once he reached his adult size. Many music stores will even apply some amount of rental payments toward the cost of a final purchase. So, we rented a violin from a store in Boston when Lauda was 9 years old. We were living in Trumball, Connecticut. When we moved to the West Coast, we bought a medium-sized violin from a store there. Years later, we purchased an adult-sized violin for Lauda.

When Shaudi wanted to move from the piano to a string instrument, we thought he might be better on the viola. After all, most middle schools have a music class, either orchestra or band. To open a child to more practice and to school-sponsored competitions, it is better to learn an instrument that is part of the school's music department. There are many violin players in the orchestra, but fewer viola and cello players. So, Shaudi began to learn the viola. Again, we had to worry about changing the instrument as he grew. However, the cost was trivial this time around. Shaudi's viola teacher suggested we repurpose Lauda's little violin frame by removing the violin strings and putting on viola strings, which are thicker and produce a lower-pitched sound. We could not tell the difference from a real viola! This worked for several years for Shaudi. When he reached his adult size, we bought a proper viola for him through his viola teacher's friend in China.

As much as our sons had shown their early interest in music, as they got older, practicing their musical instruments was one of the most contentious events in our house. It was the single most frequent cause of an unhappy relationship in the household, followed by Chinese language lessons. Each Saturday, Lauda and Shaudi would take a one-hour music lesson. We expected them to practice at home during the week, too. If they had not practiced enough at home, the next Saturday's session would be a repeat of the same fragment of music. The tuition – and the weekend time -- would not be well spent. June and I initially sat in on the lessons and took notes. We grew frustrated when we saw Lauda and Shaudi endlessly repeat the same notes. We got stricter with practice times. We told our sons they had to practice their instruments at least one hour each day, before bedtime, on the pieces they learned from both their private lessons and their school's music classes.

Both our sons rebelled against these rules, each in his own way. Lauda was so angry; he took silent "revenge" on June. One day, June saw her gold necklace, which was a present from me when I was a graduate student, broken in pieces and sitting quietly in its box, which was stored in a larger shoe box. Shaudi, meanwhile, expressed his anger on the instruments. There were many deep pencil scratches on the legs and panel of our once-nice, once-shiny piano. When we asked each of our boys what happened, neither knew how, when, or who did it. Lauda and Shaudi deployed many other tactics to reduce their practice time or avoid practicing altogether. For example, an instrument would have a broken string, so we had to wait until the weekend to have the teacher fix it.

Eventually, the hard work from them -- and us -- did produce some good results. Both Lauda and Shaudi played in their school orchestra for years, and easily fulfilled their high school graduation requirement for the arts. They also successfully auditioned for the Seattle Youth Symphony Orchestra (www.syso.org) and played there for many years. They performed in quarterly concerts. As a reward for June and me, we did not have to go anywhere else to enjoy great music. I used to say to June: "This is so good. I can't tell the difference between this and the music from the Seattle Symphony in Benaroya Hall."

June and I knew our sons would not be star musicians. They lacked self-motivation, and neither won any awards in music. In fact, both of them stopped playing their instruments publicly and privately in the later part of their high school junior year, as their school course loads increased. The violin and the viola have been collecting dust in the closet since then, though Shaudi continues to enjoy his guitar.

Lauda and Shaudi's reticence when it came to music is not unusual. After all, mastering a musical instrument is hard work. We have not heard many kids voluntarily practice for hours to learn basic notes or chords. But, it takes those hours and hours of repetition to make finger movements second nature, later allowing a musician to stand out among peers. We like to think even Yo-Yo Ma or Lang Lang had moments of rebellion against their instrument practice in their younger years. Though year after year of musical involvement should help on a college application, even if it didn't, we believe learning a musical instrument in childhood plants a seed in a child's mind, which grows into basic skills the child can use when he or she wants to pick up instruments later in their life, on their own terms. After all, when Shaudi got his guitar as a reward for academic performance, he played it a lot more willingly and happily than he had any other instrument. However, he wanted to play "his way." He declined our offer to hire a private teacher for the guitar. Thanks to his practice with the viola, though, Shaudi was able to teach himself how to play the new instrument. Lauda also asked for another instrument of his own choice to play. It was a lap harp. However, it was too difficult for Lauda to teach himself to play. We hired a private harp teacher, but Lauda's discipline for practice was still lacking. He dropped the lap harp after one semester.

Shaudi had another genuine interest of his own: drawing and painting. Though he had little patience for viola practice, Shaudi shows a meticulous and patient temperament for his artwork. We sent him to private group lessons for about one semester. He was good at it, but not good enough to win any kind of competition or award. There was no school team or local, larger organization to inspire meaningful growth. June and I debated. Should everything Shaudi does be geared for the purpose of the college application? Can he have an interest, truly his own, that we should support? We decided if our sons wanted to do something interesting to them, they could do it later in life, by themselves and from their own paycheck. Our responsibility was to raise them to be men who could stand tall and straight in society, on their own as independent adults.

Parents who do have a child who excels in any type of art – music, theater, drawing, painting, sculpture, etc. – should ensure that excellence has an outlet. Just like with sports teams, it is better if the school has an orchestra, band, art club, or theater troupe for the child to join. It is even better if the local or metropolitan area has a larger and more credible organization for the child to move up to, if he or she has a true talent in the field.

Tip: Nurture, then help your child display talent in a sector of the arts or sports via a school group, regional organization, or even national stage.

6.3. Leadership opportunities: In-school extracurricular activities and in the community opportunities

In addition to sports and arts, a well-run high school should be able to provide its students many other non-academic opportunities. This was a criterion we looked at when we moved into our school district. There should be many clubs, ranging from ones with national or international impact to those critical to the school or community.

The Key Club, for example, is an international organization that often has high school chapters. The club focuses on community service. Students volunteer for programs to help the needy, often via local organizations such as a food bank or a community shelter. Volunteering for Key Club or a similar club provides an opportunity for a student to show initiative and leadership. A student can even run for club president, treasurer, or another officer position.

The National Honor Society, founded in 1921, recognizes students who have demonstrated excellence in the areas of scholarship, leadership, service, and character. There are chapters in all 50 states, the District of Columbia, Puerto Rico, many U.S. territories, and Canada.

Of the several clubs Shaudi joined, the Key Club and the National Honor Society were both important. He frequently bought food from the grocery store to donate to local food banks. He also was a diligent member of the Crew-Link, a group that helped newcomers familiarize themselves with the school. But, Shaudi did not have an official position. When he entered these activities on his college application form, they appeared less impressive, despite the many hours he contributed. Time and energy in clubs are best rewarded if a student is in a leadership position.

---
*Tip: A student should find a school club or
activity to join, then mature into an officer role.*

Sometimes, a student can't find a club to join. The student center, the counselor's office, or the career center should have a list of clubs. Lauda looked at these clubs, but felt there was a gap. So, he followed the procedure to start a new club. He applied to the school office and provided a charter of the organization. Lauda and his friends successfully formed a new club –Fantasy Sports Club- at the school and Lauda become the founder and president. He went on to recruit more members to make the club more interesting. We noted this on his college application form.

---
*Tip: Your student can't find a compelling school club
or activity? He or she should create one!*

We encouraged both our sons to join their high school newspaper. The high school newspaper is a good place to build credentials. The editor-in-chief and section editors are highly regarded during college applications, so students who achieve these titles should list them prominently on a college application form. A mere reporter title for the paper would carry much less weight for the college application, but reporters in the freshman and sophomore classes can be promoted to editors in their junior and senior years. We read the school newspaper and found it to be informative, fun, and occasionally to include serious debates or topics. We saw that, aside from its value for college applications, serving as an editor does make a student a critical thinker and a better writer by the nature of the position. These are important traits for later life success. Despite our pleas, neither of our sons joined the newspaper staff. They were not fans of humanities courses or activities. They preferred science-oriented activities.

There are other, real life leadership roles a student can try to obtain. One such opportunity in our state is to run for a representative position on the State Board of Education. The Washington Association of Student Councils chooses two high school students each year for a two-year term. The 16-member State Board of Education is comprised of the superintendent of public instruction, five members elected by school districts from eastern and western Washington, one private school representative, seven members appointed by the governor and the two high school students. This real-life policy making experience is greatly respected by head hunters, either for a job or in a college application.

6.4. Community service

There is no limit on what community service activities a student can do outside of school. But there is no need to be too diverse here. Students shouldn't commit to multiple community service activities for a brief time and then jump to other community service activities. Instead, the wise strategy is for the student to conserve time and energy by wisely selecting one or two activities that are engaging and enjoyable for the student. This allows the student to show persistence by becoming involved in a selected activity for several years, demonstrating commitment and compassion. This service can be local or international. For example, a student can volunteer at a nursing home, hospital, homeless shelter, or Red Cross center. A student can also help disabled or special needs children in the community or at a special camp. If the student has the ability, he or she can even offer assistance in a third-world village, or even a war-torn country. These humanitarian works give back to society, serve others, and help the needy. These activities can also provide good material for writing a compassionate and detailed college essay. International works are more impressive than domestic or local community ones, but they may or may not be possible due to other commitments.

> *Tip: Make a larger impact by consolidating humanitarian into one or two consistent activities, plus international work, if possible.*

Lauda mainly did two, out-of-school volunteer activities. Both were well-thought-out and beneficial to his personal growth. The first activity spanned two consecutive summers overseas. During high school, Lauda spent two summers in China, where he set up and led an English training camp for English teachers at my old high school, in my hometown. Because this was in rural China, the high school could not recruit any formally trained English teachers. The teachers, themselves, had to learn English at night and deliver instruction to the students the next day. Their pronunciation was poor. Lauda, by contrast, could clearly understand Chinese and speak English. But how did we learn of the opportunity? Well, one summer, we visited my high school physics teacher (I always paid visits to teachers when I went back to China). My old teacher had become the high school principal. He asked if I knew of any native English-speaking teachers who were willing to do something to help his English teachers improve their skills. When I came back to the United States, I asked around but could not find any volunteers to help. I admit, I also felt uneasy to ask anyone unfamiliar with the area to go through the hardships in my hometown, as did Lauda. Finally, I asked Lauda to do this task and he agreed. It was a good international volunteering experience for Lauda, both for his personal growth as well as his college application. The trips also provided great material for writing his long college essay, as shown in Chapter 7.

The second of Lauda's two out-of-school, volunteer activities involved the laboratory research at the Fred Hutchinson Cancer Research Center as mentioned above under the guidance of a family friend who happened to be a scientist there. After consulting with his laboratory director, our friend agreed to take on Lauda. It is not easy to accept the responsibility of teaching a high school student. The supervisor must spend his valuable time training the student, then must watch the student's work for the first few weeks. Once the student has developed the skills to conduct experiments, the student may or may not contribute to the main project of the laboratory. Results then need to be repeated by the supervisor.

To enable him to work in the lab, Lauda had an early dismissal from high school every Thursday. June would drive him to the research center, spending 40 minutes in rush hour traffic. Lauda would spend about three hours in the lab. Then, on Saturday, June would drive Lauda to the lab again to spend four hours there. The seven hours a week meant 28 hours a month, or an impressive 280 hours over the 10-month school year. Lauda did this for about two years. He did learn useful biological research skills, which helped his application and, later, his research work for his senior honor thesis at Stanford University. As mentioned earlier, one of the Ivy League colleges offered him not only an admission but also multi-summer research grants and a five-year master's degree track, and we believed that offer was due to the recognition of Lauda's research experience. The experience lasted in other ways, too: Lauda still likes to do research and wants to be involved in scientific investigations.

In fact, Lauda's keen interest in laboratory research has been lifelong. From age two, Lauda had been around laboratories. When Lauda was a toddler, he and June joined me in London, England, where I was doing my Ph.D. thesis on cancer immunology at the Royal Postgraduate Medical School/Hammersmith Hospital. I spent most of my time in the laboratory for the three years my family was in London. The three of us lived in a graduate student apartment across the street from the research building. After dinner, Lauda would come and stay in the laboratory. He played with the microscope, or pipetting, sometimes pretending to work in the hood with the sterile cell cultures. When my family and I moved to Vancouver, Canada, where I did my postdoctoral fellowship at a cancer agency, we, again, lived near my work. In fact, Lauda's most frequent outing after school was to the research laboratory. He liked to feed the fish I used for extracting DNA for cloning a unique cancer gene.

In contrast to Lauda, Shaudi had very little early exposure to research. With our next move to Bethesda, Maryland, when Shaudi was only three months old, I continued research work at the National Institutes of Health as a staff scientist. But, my family and I lived 40 minutes away from this laboratory. The children occasionally visited my work over the weekend but, in contrast to Lauda's keen interest, Shaudi would just go to sleep in his stroller. In addition, Shaudi did not have a chance to visit the laboratory for long periods, as his brother had. When Shaudi was three and a half, I stopped my research career and moved on to clinical work.

So, Shaudi didn't perform research, but he still completed regular community service at our local cancer treatment clinic. Instead of conducting experiments like his brother, Shaudi interacted directly with patients. Like Lauda, Shaudi took early dismissal on Thursdays and would spend about three hours every week in the clinic. However, during the winter and autumn months, the dismal weather and Shaudi's tennis practices and competitions often interfered with his ability to volunteer. Still, he accumulated hundreds of hours at the clinic during his high school years. Shaudi helped to comfort patients by delivering snacks and drinks, and he assisted the nurses by gathering supplies.

Shaudi also interacted with patients internationally. From the time he started high school, Shaudi spent every summer doing volunteer work in China. When visiting my home in rural China, I always provided free medical services and had been doing so ever since my graduation from medical school. As a certified doctor from America, more and more patients came from far away to seek a "magic cure." Noting the growing needs of my fellow countryside people, I recruited my office staff to form medical teams to do volunteer work in my village. Naturally, Shaudi had seen many of these activities and joined the efforts to help others in need. Again, this turned out to be a great experience for Shaudi, not only for his college application but also for his personal growth. The descriptions of his activities were truly touching, as shown in Chapters 7 and 11. Like Lauda's lifelong affection for research, Shaudi continued his humanitarian efforts even after he went to college.

Tip: To best benefit the community in need, volunteer work should stem from a student's interests.

June and I felt both of our sons had learned humility from their international volunteer experience. There were so many less fortunate people around the world. We could have been among those who suffered, and, for that matter, Lauda and Shaudi would have been among those less fortunate if not for the hard work and good luck of their parents. My sons do not look down on the poor, the disabled, the ill, and the disadvantaged. Neither has ever complained about the harsh life and the tough living environment they experienced in China. They ate noodles every day, slept on a hard-board bed, toileted in trenches dug into the ground, and were bitten so profusely by mosquitoes that they got itchy, red bumps all over their body. In other words, they lived just like everyone else in the village. Still, Lauda and Shaudi made the trip back each year. In contrast, some children of my relatives, who were born and grew up in the cities in China, rarely return to the village because the old home is "too dirty and too poor."

We know other students who did volunteer work in Africa, Haiti, and other natural disaster-ridden countries. These are truly beneficial experience for a young person growing up in America. From these trips, American students gain appreciation of what they have and what they can do to help others. To us, even if it is not to enhance a college application, it is still worthwhile for parents to look out for opportunities like this for their students. If a parent cannot find a way to fund an international trip, students should still offer community service close to home. For example, both Lauda and Shaudi volunteered time at the Hope-Link food service center. The hours were not enough to report on their application forms, but they were still worthwhile to our sons' development.

Tip: Beyond college applications, volunteer work should help students become better people and more appreciative of their own good fortune.

As Elizabeth Wissner-Gross stated in her book *What Colleges Don't Tell You (And Other Parents Don't Want You to Know):* "Do not let the students waste the summer break 'hanging-out.' Summer activities often provide defining moments and grist for essays."

Chapter 7. The Long and Short College Admission Essays

7.1. The Long College Essay

As shown by the importance of the high school GPA and tests such as the SAT and ACT, the American college admissions process has a scientific approach. However, admission decisions also have strong subjective elements that are out of a student's control. No matter how impressive a student's grades, test scores and extracurricular activities may be, college or university acceptance also relies on some personal feelings by admissions officers. These people often review many applications from brilliant students. Therefore, they must make decisions using criteria in addition to numbers. A major criterion is often an essay.

The importance of the essay can take two forms. First, it can improve the odds for a student who is mathematically close, but not assured, a spot at a high-profile university. One admissions officer explained this scenario: "A great essay could heal the sick, but could not raise the dead." The second form of the personal essay's importance is improving the odds for a student who is mathematically impressive to gain admission to a high-profile university. This is necessary because many excellent students, even those with top GPAs and SAT scores, can be rejected by highly selective colleges. In fact, as mentioned earlier, it was once a trend for these colleges to reject high-scoring students.

So, since top grades and test scores alone do not combine to guarantee a welcome letter from an admissions officer, a student must attempt to connect with the admissions officer via an application's personal essays. These writing strategies work. A few years ago, admissions deans rated the essay the third most important factor in their decision whether to accept or reject a student. Yes, test scores and

GPA ranked higher. But, ranking below the personal essay were recommendation letters and extra-curricular activities.

<hr>
Tip: Once test scores and high school grades are the best they can be, essays can make the admissions difference for a range of students.
<hr>

The main goal of the college essay is to reveal the personal side of the applicant beyond the cold, hard grades and test scores. These essays should convey an intimate and lively portrait of the applicant, and provide insight into who the applicant is. There are many books and articles on how to write a great college essay. As Dr. Katherine Cohen more elegantly stated in her book *Rock Hard Application*[5]: "It is through the personal essay that the application becomes a living, breathing document of one's achievements, success and failures, trials, tribulations, hopes and dreams. It is the proxy, the spokesperson, the ambassador, and an engaging conversation between the applicant and the college admission officers." We read Dr. Cohen's book and several others during Lauda and Shaudi's application processes. One book produced by the Princeton Review[4] was particularly useful in that it listed samples of real essays. We asked our sons to read the books too.

A college or university admissions officer expects a high school student to write a good, mature essay to reveal his or her true self. The substance and storylines should illustrate the student's personality, character, and passion. The student should accomplish this through stories, not statements.

<hr>
Tip: The best essays are narratives that show the admissions officer how the student is a living, breathing person, not just a compilation of test scores and high school grades.
<hr>

"Despite advancing years, people tend to retain many childhood likes and dislikes," explained one admissions officer. "People never seem to tire of 'storytime.'"

In other words, show via anecdote, don't tell via example; and, when showing, use showmanship. Katherine Cohen, Ph.D., explains this writing concept in her book, *The Truth About Getting In*[6].

"The essay topic should be specific in detail yet universal in theme, attention-grabbing in tone yet methodical in structure," Cohen wrote. "It is a story that reads dramatically and with a solid, clear structure."

The material for a student's well-told story can come from summer jobs or volunteer experience or other extra-curricular activities. But, to find substance, the student must be deeply engaged in the activity. Simply showing up at a homeless shelter is nice, but not enough. The student must pay attention, see detail, and become truly involved. So, connecting with the needs, concerns, and desires of a person or people who work or stay at the homeless shelter would make a better essay. Fiction is unlikely to be acceptable. Some students have tried poems, but poetry probably won't be appreciated by a non-poetically inclined admissions officer. Both Lauda and Shaudi stuck to the old style of using real, unique experience to provide their storylines. The final essays were touching and impressive, especially Shaudi's.

Lauda used his experience from the summer English training class in China to answer the prompt *"Attach a picture and describe its significance to you."*

(*The final version*): As I stepped off the Boeing 767, I was blasted by a nostalgic wave of hot, humid air. It was then that I truly realized that I had arrived. My purpose in coming to China was to teach English classes at my father's old high school. However, I was not quite at my destination. From Shanghai, my dad and I caught a train to the province of Henan. Because we were unable to secure tickets for a sleeper train, we bought seat tickets and sat through a nighttime eighteen-hour journey. I wasn't able to fall asleep at all, even with my jet lag, because the train operators left the fluorescent lights on and crowds of passengers were milling around. The train was so overbooked that even getting to the restroom was a huge effort. I had to squeeze between the people who only bought "standing tickets." In comparison, I was lucky to be able to sit down. We arrived the next afternoon at my dad's hometown of Baofeng. The high school offered us an unused dorm to sleep in, but it only had one bed so I had to improvise. Taking a bamboo mat and old sheets, I fashioned a makeshift sleeping bag. Even with the extremely loud air conditioner and my allergies to the moldy sheets, I fell asleep because I was so exhausted. Still, I did not forget my commitment; my first lesson would start at seven o'clock the next morning.

At Yi Gao High School, there are fifteen teachers in the English department for two thousand students. It is hard for this rural school to recruit formally trained English teachers with precise pronunciations. They must make do with what they have. As a junior, I was invited to coordinate a summer class in order to improve the Yi Gao English teachers' oral speech. Thus, I planned lessons that would be discussion-based, contrary to the traditional Chinese method of lecture and homework. I used pre-made PowerPoint slides and DVDs to try to elicit discussion. Unfortunately for me, the teachers were shy and did not take easily to public speaking. That summer's lessons were tedious and somewhat frustrating, but I felt that I had accomplished much so I made a commitment to return the following year. This time, returning as a mature and experienced senior, I implemented a more lenient lesson plan. I knew that I was better prepared this time, but I still felt a little queasy when I woke at six to get ready for my lessons. Armed with a camcorder and voice recorder, I entered the classroom. I saw some returning faces, but there were just as many newcomers. I still felt uneasy facing these adults. They were able to take time out of their busy lives in order to take a class from a high schooler. I felt the pressure and obligation to put forth my best effort. After all-around introductions, I eased into my designed lesson. Each teacher would give an impromptu three-minute speech about whatever topic the class chose. However, the teachers still did not feel comfortable being put in the spotlight. As the week progressed, I realized that I had to modify my original teaching plan. With help from the teachers, I explored the best strategies to teach most efficiently. Eventually, we settled into a pattern of read, record, and review. Using their lesson books, they read off a list of vocabulary words and a short story as I recorded them. I would then replay the tape and correct any faulty pronunciations to the class. Interestingly, a few of them just could not distinguish between the pronunciations of "fire" and "fare." I had to lead them in practice many times every day until they finally pronounced the words correctly. To loosen up the tension and add a fun aspect to the lessons, I would bring up various tongue twisters. Amusing for us here in the States, it was also humorous in China when even I struggled to pronounce the tricky phrases. When the week of lessons ended, I was very aware of their improvement. As I bid farewell to them that afternoon, I felt the gratification in knowing that my goal had been achieved.

My father had received a solid education from this school, which in turn led to his success in his career. He believes that he needs to repay his hometown for all that it did for him. Having heard his frequent quotation of "much is given, much is expected," I decided that I should contribute as well. While he was in the nearby villages providing medical advice, I was at his high school teaching English. What I did was not a big deal for me, but it meant a lot to the teachers and students of this rural town. Some of the teachers even brought their children to my lessons. It was inspiring to see these adults making the best out of this opportunity. I was especially amazed to see a journalist and a news crew in my classroom one morning. They heard about my lessons and wanted to do a piece about what I did. This reemphasized the community's appreciation for what I did, even if I didn't realize it then. My experiences in China have strengthened my belief that everyone is useful and important. Each person has his own talent to contribute to the world. I recognize now the hardships of the students in China; not every educational resource is of the highest quality and easily accessible. I have learned to make the most out of every opportunity because valuable ones come very rarely. It is crucial to realize that life gives us the ability to do whatever we want. In the end, it is up to the individual to take that chance.

Of course, Lauda did not simply sit down and write his essay. There were hours and hours of hard work involved. He had a first draft and ten sets of revisions. This was his first draft:

(*The first draft*): As I stepped off the 767, I was blasted by a nostalgic wave of hot, humid air. It was then that I truly realized that I arrived in China. My purpose here was to teach English classes for a week at my dad's old high school. However, I was not quite at my destination. From Shanghai, my dad and I caught a train to the Henan province. Because we weren't able to secure tickets for a sleeper train, we had to sit on the bench seats. I wasn't able to fall asleep at all, even with jet lag, because the train operators were obnoxious enough to leave the florescent lights on. The trains are overbooked in order to boost operating revenue so it was as packed as possible. Even to get to the bathroom, I had to go through countless crowded compartments and squeeze between the people who only bought "standing tickets." In reminiscence, I was very lucky to be able to sit down and rest. When the 18 hours of misery terminated at my dad's hometown of Baofeng, I finally saw my paternal relatives again. However, we had to find a place to stay until we received accommodations. The high school offered us an unused dorm to sleep in. It had only one bed so I had to improvise. Taking a bamboo mat and old sheets, I made a makeshift sleeping bag. Even with the extremely loud air conditioner and allergies to the moldy sheets, I fell because I was exhausted and sleep deprived. I knew that tomorrow would be my first lesson two floors above me, but I had not forgotten what I originally promised to do: teach English.

Because accents are a big problem for the people here, I decided to focus solely on spoken English. What they learned from me would help their students learn a more-natural English. From last year's experience, I knew that this year was not going to be easy either. Armed with a camcorder and voice recorder, my dad and I taught the class with a less rigorous lesson plan. As I entered the classroom, I saw some returning faces, but there were more newcomers. What still discomforted me were their ages. Some students were around the same age as my father. They were able to take time out of their busy lives to take an English class from a high schooler. We started by making introductions all around. I wanted the class to realize that this would be a discussion-based class, contrary to the traditional Chinese method of lecture and homework. I had to establish the fact that they were the important people here. We, the English teachers, meant nothing. As the week progressed, the lessons varied depending on what the class wanted to do, whichever way would help them learn best. Eventually, we settled into a pattern of read, record, and review. They would read off a list of vocabulary words, and we would record them and then correct them. To make things interactive, I would bring up various tongue twisters. We all had fun doing those. Since last year, our class drew more attention from the public. The newspaper did an article about the class, and we were even in a local news broadcast. Most importantly, we had more students. Some of these teachers even brought their children to the lessons, to try to give them a head start on their English. It was inspiring to see these adults trying to make better lives for their children. Many can say that children are the future, but here, I saw this maxim in practice.

Interestingly, the principal at this school was my dad's old English teacher. My father had received a firm foundation in English from this teacher, which in turn led to his success in college. He believes that he needs to repay this debt by volunteering his time at his former high school. The reason I went back was to help the people improve their lives. The students in China do not all have top-notch English teachers, thus their learned English is not necessarily the best. Because English is a very important language in this modern era, Chinese students need to concentrate on learning the language well. My job is to help them along this path. With a solid English foundation, they can attend foreign colleges and receive a better-specialized education, as did my father.

Lauda wrote that first draft during the first few weeks of the summer after his junior year. Starting early allowed him plenty of time to work on his writing. With each revision came visible improvement.

During this process, June and I were eager to offer suggestions. Lauda took some of our ideas, but, when it was his turn to write his college entrance essay, Shaudi was resistant.

"I'm not a very good writer, but I'm an excellent rewriter," Shaudi would explain, citing the famous James Michener quote to stop me whenever I was about to comment on his essay. This was actually progress. In the summer after his junior year, Shaudi showed us the first draft and believed it was good enough and he was done with this task. Shaudi ended up with half as many essay drafts as Lauda had created, but his revisions did help. His prompt was "*Evaluate a significant experience, achievement, risk you have taken, or ethical dilemma you have faced and its impact on you.*" Here is his first draft:

As I got off the plane and crossed the bridge into the main terminal, I entered a world that I did not recognize. Though I had come to this same country the year before for the same purpose and with the same intentions, I still was not accustomed to the transition that came with this trip. Every year since 8th grade, my father, an oncologist, and I fly back to China to provide medical care for his home-village in Baofeng of the Henan province where his mother still resides. His rationale is that "you must give back to the society that raised you." Last year we brought along two of my dad's American co-workers, both experienced in the field of medicine. It's an intimidating feeling knowing that in a country of over 1.3 billion people, there are only three people with whom you can readily communicate.

We were picked up by an old friend of my father's who gave us all a hearty welcome while I replied with a very American accented, "ni hao." We spent the next few days touring famous attractions, before we took a thirteen hour train ride from Beijing to Baofeng. When I looked out from my bed situated on the top level, it was then that I truly appreciated my comfort. I saw the rows of passengers who did not have the same luxury as I, who could not afford a bed-ticket and had to endure an overnight trip with only overhanging handles to grasp.

At Baofeng, my father's sister and her husband drove us to the village. The world melted away before my eyes; in this trip that lasted only 30 minutes, the lighted malls soon turned into crumbled buildings, the gas powered cars morphed into wagons pulled by mules, the shops into vagabond fruit and vegetables stands, and enormous crop fields stretched endlessly. The essence of two worlds so different cannot be properly captured under one name. Pulling into my father's former residence, I finally began to feel a sense of belonging as many things became familiar to me. I recognized my grandmother's wrinkles, the crumbling walls of the estate, the toilet which was essentially a hole in the ground, the prodding lumps from my mattress, and the inquisitive buzzing of frustrated mosquitoes trying to find a way through my mosquito net. Once again, I spent my nights in the very antithesis of what I had been accustomed to all of my life.

I wanted to sleep in and I could have, but a sense of duty made me climb out of my bed. We had time to dine on a simple breakfast of bread and plain porridge before heading to our respective tasks. My dad and one of the Americans traveled to a local run-down hospital to give a talk about diabetes awareness while over the next few days, the other co-worker and I stayed in the village and performed blood pressure and blood sugar tests on countless villagers. One day consisted of upwards of five hours of testing and almost one hundred patients. By the end of each day, my ears throbbed with pain from the stethoscope, but for some reason I still put it back on, perhaps for the same reason I pushed myself out of bed each of those days.

However, it was the patients who had the greatest impact on me. I remember their hands calloused from working in the field, hardened to the extent that I could not prick their fingers and draw blood for blood sugar testing. If only ear pain were the sole hardship they had to endure. I vividly remember an incident where a patient was wheeled in on a wagon to the front entrance. She was paralyzed from a stroke and the family was seeking our help. I am a mere teenager without any idea of how to say 'stroke' or 'thrombolytic therapy' in Chinese, and my partner had no way of communicating to the locals other than through me. We did not know how to respond as the family eagerly looked at us, waiting for an answer, or maybe a better term would be, 'cure.' Standing there clueless, something became apparent to me. All these patients sought a panacea; they believed that America had the answer to their ailments and we could magically cure their diseases, and I understood their thoughts. Faced with such an arduous lifestyle, they do not lead lives that stop for medical issues. They wanted an easy solution because this was their one opportunity for treatment. I kept this thought with me as I boarded the plane and very much like the scenery outside of that car window, I, too, had changed. I saw things that some people will never know and some know all too well. I finally understood the true meaning of my father's statement.

Even from the first draft, we knew Shaudi's essay had potential. The words he used were beautiful, and the flow of the sentences was flawless, just like the work of a mature writer. But the essay lacked substance, facts, or details for the main message. A contentious few months in our household followed. I had to bring out my published books, Ph.D. thesis, and many scientific papers to show Shaudi I had sufficient credentials to qualify me to make suggestions for a college entrance essay.

Shaudi still refused to accept my advice.

One day, I came across Mark Twain's famous piece about the wisdom of fathers: "When I was a boy of 14, my father was so ignorant I could hardly stand to have the old man around. But when I got to be 21, I was astonished at how much the old man had learned in seven years." I was awakened!

"Ah-ha, it is the teenage thing," I told June. "I need to revise my strategy when dealing with Shaudi."

I stopped telling Shaudi what to do. Instead, I encouraged him to show his essay to friends who were already in college, his teachers, or a supervisor at his summer camp. When Shaudi showed me his essay again, I could see he made some fine revisions based on the suggestions of these editors. If June or I had any suggestions, we would detour the message through Lauda to Shaudi, as if the suggestions were from Lauda. Lauda was at the age when he was capable of appreciating the wisdom of his parents, and Shaudi was at the age when he was capable of appreciating the wisdom of his older brother. The result was this fifth draft:

140...160...180 mmHg. I stopped squeezing the pump and carefully turned the metal wheel between my thumb and forefinger, listening intently over the whistle of air as the needle wound down to 0. I repeated the process again. 140, 160, 180...0. Couldn't get it. Again, 140, 160, 180...0. Still nothing. Why couldn't I get this patient's blood pressure? I was puzzled.

Every summer since the 8th grade, I have returned to Baofeng in Henan, China as part of a small medical team led by my father to provide free basic medical care in the rural villages where his many relatives still reside. Having observed the villagers' poor health and limited access to care during my childhood visits there, I was aware of the great need for this service. Naturally, I was excited to become part of the team to aid the people as much as my abilities allowed.

After landing in Beijing from a 12-hour flight, we took a 13-hour train ride to Baofeng. The train's sleeper-tickets were sold-out so we bought seat-tickets for the ride. Even with sleep deprivation from the plane trip, dozing off was a challenge made more difficult by the noxious fumes of smokers and uncomfortable seats. Despite these conditions, my situation was still "luxurious". I saw rows of passengers who could afford neither bed nor sitting ticket and instead endured an overnight trip standing. What caught my attention was how complacent they appeared, which made me see how fortunate I was. But in a few hours I would see many more that were even less fortunate.

Upon arriving, we immediately went to our respective tasks with only a short break to rest and recover; we wasted little time getting our care to the people who needed it. One team traveled to the local, poorly-supported hospitals to discuss diabetes awareness while I stayed with another team at the de facto clinic we set up in a communal area near my grandmother's hut. Soon, a line of patients snaked through the corridors of the village as we performed blood pressure and glucose tests on countless villagers. Thus started my two-week health mission.

One strenuous day consisted of seven hours of testing over one hundred patients. My ears throbbed with pain from the stethoscope, but I put it back on. For many, this was the first check-up of their lifetime, and for some, they would find out they were diabetic or hypertensive despite never having heard these words before.

140, 160, 180...0mmHg. As the summer sun blazed above and sweat dripped down my cheek, my left hand robotically wiped the perspiration while my right continued to pump the sphygmomanometer. I listened for an initial sound but instantly received a barrage of beats that quickly ceased. The result was always the same. Confused, I consulted a team member, a Registered Nurse. She discovered that my inability to get a reading was caused by the patient's extreme blood pressure: 220/140, a hypertensive emergency. The patient was given medications that we had brought with us. On the next day for his follow-up, I had a much easier time with the examination: 140/90. The team physician patted me on the back for my perseverance in preventing "a potentially life threatening stroke". It was then that I understood the reality and seriousness of what I was doing.

I felt my patients' hands calloused from working in the fields, hardened to the extent that I could barely prick their fingers to draw blood for testing. I vividly remember an incident in which a patient who was paralyzed from a stroke was brought in on a homemade wheelchair. Her eyes were dim and void of spirit, her face just as lifeless. The family eagerly looked at us, waiting for an answer. I had no idea of how to say 'stroke' or 'thrombolytic therapy' in Chinese, and my partners had no way of communication other than through me. I had thought that my CPR certification and glucose training would prepare me sufficiently for this trip. I was clearly wrong. Wanting to do the most I could, I tested her glucose level which came out to be very low. We told the family to feed her some candy when they got home and our physician would contact them to adjust her medications. They came back the next day for re-examination; her eyes had an unseen brightness and her face, a livelier expression. The family showered us with thanks, offering to treat us to dinner (the highest local social honor) despite financial hardship, and pleading that we stay longer. I thought that we did not do much for the patient as her limbs were still paralyzed, but the family did not feel the same way. They praised us for bringing life back into her, convincing me that small things really can make a difference and for the first time, I felt that I had sincerely made an impact, a feeling with which I had been unfamiliar before taking part of this annual medical trip.

When our time in the village was done, much like the eyes of my patient and the scenery outside that car window, I, too, had changed. I entered China not knowing what to expect but left enriched by the experiences accumulated from my many trips. No longer a passive bystander, I took a more active role and I now truly understand the need for this service having seen the condition of the villagers and personally being touched by them. Holding the hundreds of hands hardened by hours of commitment to land and home, my appreciation for the contributions of my fellow human beings grew immensely. As a caregiver, my patients showed me that we are all uniquely valuable. Each summer, I eagerly look to return to Baofeng because I know that I can make a difference in other people's lives.

This version lost the beautiful words and sentences describing the scenery shift, but Shaudi had to remove them because the essay was getting too long. But, he more than made up for that loss by adding more details, and an opening sentence that was more intriguing and attention-getting.

The final version of Shaudi's essay as shown below is a touching story, even to this date my eyes still get wet when I read it. It reminded me of the suffering and the great need of those patients, and brought the vivid scene of our workday there to my mind.

140...160...180mmHg. I stopped squeezing the pump and carefully turned the metal wheel between my thumb and forefinger, listening intently over the whistle of air as the needle wound down to 0. I repeated the process again. 140, 160, 180...0. Couldn't get it. Again: 140, 160, 180...0. Still nothing. Why couldn't I get this patient's blood pressure? I was puzzled.

For every summer since the 8th grade, I have returned to China as part of a small medical team led by my father. We provide free, basic medical care for the rural villages of Baofeng in the Henan province where he spent his childhood and many of our relatives still reside. Having observed the villagers' poor health and limited access to care during my childhood visits there, I was aware of the great need for this service. Naturally, I was eager to become part of the team to aid the people as much as I could.

During my first trip, we spent 25 continuous hours traveling; after landing in Beijing from a 12-hour flight, we took a 13-hour train ride to Baofeng. Since the train's sleeper-tickets were sold-out we had to buy seat-tickets for the ride. Even with sleep deprivation from the plane trip, dozing off was a challenge made more difficult by the noxious fumes of smokers and uncomfortable seats. Despite these conditions, my situation was still quite "luxurious". I saw rows of passengers who could afford neither bed nor sitting ticket and instead endured an overnight trip standing. What caught my attention was how complacent they appeared which made me see how fortunate I was, but in a few hours I would see many more that were even less fortunate.

Upon arriving, we immediately went to our respective tasks. One team traveled to the local, poorly-supported hospitals to discuss diabetes awareness while I stayed with the other team at the de facto clinic we set up in a communal area near my grandmother's hut. Soon, a line of patients snaked through the muddy corridors of the village as we performed blood pressure and glucose tests on countless villagers. Thus started my two-week health mission.

Every day consisted of seven hours of testing over one hundred patients. My ears continuously throbbed with pain from the stethoscope, but for each patient I put it back on. My discomfort paled in comparison to the hardships that these villagers experienced on a daily basis. For many, this was the first check-up of their lifetime, and for some, they would find out they were diabetic or hypertensive despite never having heard these words before.

140, 160, 180…0mmHg. As the summer sun blazed above and sweat dripped down my cheeks, my left hand robotically wiped the perspiration while my right continued to pump the sphygmomanometer. I listened for an initial beat but instead received a barrage of beats that ceased as quickly as they had started. No matter how many times I repeated the process, I kept on hearing this barrage of beats. Confused, I consulted a team member, a Registered Nurse. She discovered that my inability to get a reading was caused by the patient's extreme blood pressure, 220/140, that was beyond the limit for which I had been testing. This signaled a hypertensive emergency, so the patient was immediately given medications that we had brought with us. The patient came back the next day for reexamination: 140/90. The team physician patted me on the back for my perseverance in preventing "a potentially life threatening stroke". It was then that I understood the reality and seriousness of what I was doing.

I remember feeling my patients' hands calloused from working in the fields, hardened to the extent that I could barely prick their fingers to draw blood for testing. I vividly recall another incident two summers ago in which a patient who was paralyzed from a stroke was brought in on a homemade wheelchair made from knotted bamboo and wheels taken from a wagon. Her eyes were dim and void of spirit, her face just as lifeless. The family eagerly looked at us, waiting for a cure to her ailment. I had no idea of how to say 'stroke' or 'thrombolytic therapy' in Chinese, and my partners had no way of communication other than through me. I had thought that my CPR certification and glucose test training would prepare me sufficiently for this trip. I was clearly wrong; they were looking for something that I could not give them. Wanting to do the most I could, I tested her glucose level which came out to be very low. We told the family to feed her some candy when they got home, and our physician would contact them to prescribe a medication regiment. They came later that day for re-examination; her eyes had an unseen brightness and her face, a livelier expression. The family showered us with thanks, offering to treat us to dinner (the highest local social honor) despite financial hardship. I thought that we didn't really do much for the patient because her limbs were still paralyzed, but the family did not feel the same way. They praised us for bringing life back into her, convincing me that small things really can make a difference. Standing there, I felt that I had sincerely made an impact, a feeling with which I had been unfamiliar before taking part in this annual medical trip.

Our time in the village eventually came to a close. Much like the eyes of my patient, I, too, had changed. Each time, I entered China not knowing what to expect but left enriched by the experiences accumulated from my many trips. No longer a passive bystander, I took a more active role, and I now truly understand the need for this service having seen the condition of the villagers and personally being touched by them. Holding the hundreds of hands hardened by hours of commitment to land and home, my appreciation for the contributions of my fellow human beings grew immensely. As a caregiver, I've been shown by my patients that we are all uniquely valuable. Each summer, I eagerly look to return to Baofeng because I know that I can make a difference in other people's lives. However, I always keep in mind that the true reason for my actions comes from the fact that there is still much to be done.

From both Lauda and Shaudi's writing experiences, we learned that the last paragraph is often the most difficult part of the writing. It should summarize the story with reflections and lessons learned. These reflections will raise the level of maturity, bring out the character, and show the passion of the student. If you would go back to read the essay again, you would realize that it is the last paragraph that elevate the level of the essay. The next two long essays from Tsong, son of a close family friend gained early decision acceptance from University of Pennsylvania, further illustrate the importance of the last paragraph.

(First draft) Strolling along the coast of the Pacific Ocean near sunset, I marvel at the beautiful symphony of the sun, ocean, sky, and the cool breeze that gently caresses both my mind and body. I feel... peaceful. I close my eyes, and suddenly I see a 13-year-old boy with black hair and glasses. He oddly seems both familiar and strange; I cannot tell. As I look upon him more closely, I am startled to find confusion and fear in his brown eyes; I am even shocked to realize that boy was me, the old me. I have not talked to him for a long time; I almost forgot who he is. As I began to approach him, I relived the bittersweet story.

Perhaps it was my doubts about coming to the U.S. or just me being a blithe kid in middle school. I was quite apathetic about the news that my family was actually moving to the U.S. in the summer of 2008. I thought I would be just fine. I was so sure that everything would be okay; so sure, like Einstein claimed that "God does not play dice." Well, after the first month of September, I was more uncertain than the particles in quantum dynamics.

I barely knew any English or anything about the school. I tried to be nonchalant about it, but I was completely petrified. Having trouble opening my locker on the first day, I realized this was not going to be easy. For me, lunch time seemed interminable; seeing everyone else talking and laughing about something that I could not even possibly comprehend. This made me realize that I was indeed alone. If traveling at the speed of light can create time dilations, then what loneliness creates is the ultimate dimension of despair. For the first couple of months in the U.S., uncertainty and doubt flooded my mind: Why is life so difficult? What do I do? And ultimately, who am I?

One night on the weekend, I overheard my mom on the phone with dad who is constantly in China because of business. She talked about how things were going for us, and all of a sudden, she started sobbing. She said she did not know what to do, and she is alone. Standing outside of her bedroom, I froze and felt as if my head was spinning. I wanted to comfort her and tell whom I love the most that everything would get better. I could not! I did not have the courage or the qualifications; I was not strong enough to escape loneliness. Tears trickled down my cheeks against my will; they tasted salty and bitter. I silently swore to beat all the odds. I need to and must be strong for my mother and for myself.

With that promise in my mind, I transferred to a new school in ninth grade. I figured that this was a chance to try something new. I forced myself to face my worst fear: writing and speaking English. With anxiety, I started to talk to my 9th grade English teacher, Mr. Lenocker, about school, books and my life. I was amazed by his knowledge, vision, and words. The anxiety gradually turned into delight as we shared our thoughts about world affairs, George Orwell's Animal Farm, and our life stories. Mr. Lenocker, a man in his mid-50's who quit his job as a manager at Microsoft to be a teacher, said one thing that opened my tightly-shut eyes: "It's not the way things are, but it's the way that we make them to be." Choice, it is choice that differentiates people. I could make a choice to change my life. I chose to master English; I chose to get involved in school activities; I chose to make friends; I chose to make my family proud; I chose to be the best I can be. Well, who am I? I am a man who chooses and accepts.

85

The night of my 17th birthday, my mother embraced me and said in her accented English, "You make me proud." I put my arms around her and I let tears come down. This time, they tasted sweet.

This is a good life story and you can feel the pain and agony that young Tsong had to endure in his early life. But you also feel the abrupt ending of the story and the sense of lost in thinking. At the suggestion of his counselors Tsong then revised his essay slightly as following.

(*Final draft*) Strolling along the coast of the Pacific Ocean near sunset, I marvel at the beautiful symphony of the sun, ocean, sky, and the cool breeze that gently caresses both my mind and body. I feel... peaceful. I close my eyes, and suddenly I see a 13-year-old boy with black hair and glasses. He oddly seems both familiar and strange; I cannot tell. As I look upon him more closely, I am startled to find confusion and fear in his brown eyes; I am even shocked to realize that the boy is me, the old me. I have not talked to him for a long time; I almost forget who he is. As I begin to approach him, I relive the bittersweet story.

Perhaps it was my doubts about coming to the U.S. or just me being a blithe kid in middle school. I was quite apathetic about the news that my family was actually moving to the U.S. in the summer of 2008. I thought I would be just fine. I was so sure that everything would be okay; so sure, like Einstein claimed that "God does not play dice." Well, after the first month of September, I was more uncertain than the particles in quantum dynamics.

I barely knew any English or anything about the school. I tried to be nonchalant about it, but I was completely petrified. Having trouble opening my locker on the first day, I realized this was not going to be easy. Lunch time seemed interminable; seeing everyone else talking and laughing about something that I could not even comprehend. This made me realize that I was indeed alone. If traveling at the speed of light can create time dilations, then what loneliness creates is the ultimate dimension of despair. For the first couple of months in the U.S., uncertainty and doubt flooded my mind: Why is life so difficult? What do I do? And ultimately, who am I?

One night, I overheard my mom on the phone with dad who was constantly in China because of business. She talked about how things were going for us, and all of a sudden, she started sobbing. She said she did not know what to do, and she is alone. Standing outside of her bedroom, I froze and felt as if my head was spinning. I wanted to comfort her and tell whom I love the most that everything would get better. I could not! I did not have the courage or the qualifications; I was not strong enough to escape loneliness. Tears trickled down my cheeks against my will; they tasted salty and bitter. I silently swore to beat all the odds. I need to and must be strong for my mother and for myself.

With that promise in my mind, I transferred to a new school in ninth grade. I figured that this was a chance to try something new. I forced myself to face my worst fear: writing and speaking English. With anxiety, I started to talk to my 9th grade English teacher, Mr. Lenocker, about school, books and my life. I was amazed by his knowledge, vision, and words. The anxiety gradually turned into delight as we shared our thoughts about world affairs, George Orwell's Animal Farm, and our life stories. Mr. Lenocker, a man in his mid-50's who quit his job as a manager at Microsoft to be a teacher, said one thing that opened my tightly-shut eyes: "It's not the way things are, but it's the way that we make them to be." Choice, it is choice that differentiates people. I could make a choice to change my life. I chose to master English; I chose to get involved in school activities; I chose to make friends; I chose to become a leader; I chose to be the best I can be. Well, who am I? I am a man who chooses and accepts, a man who is defined by unwavering determination.

At the dinner of a family gathering for my 17th birthday, I quietly reflected on my journey in the US. It is a complicated journey filled with tears and pain, but not without joy and accomplishment. This invaluable experience will accompany me for the rest of my life, reminding me that obstacles are inexorable, but I can choose to overcome, and I will! I stood up from the table and thanked my mother for her sacrifices and pain for my personal growth; she embraced me and said in her accented English, "You make me proud." I put my arms around her and I let tears come down. This time, they tasted sweet.

With mere addition of a few more sentences to the last paragraph, a strong determined character and a positive personality of the writer is revealed; and the level of sophistication and maturity of the essay is elevated to a very much different height.

From their writing experiences, we learned our sons, and majority of high school students, did have the capability to write better essays, if pushed to their potential. But if left to their own desires, they would not have continued beyond the first version of their essays. Those would have been weak pieces of work. Having good material available to write about was the first step. The second step is creating a good essay about that material.

Tip: Once a student finds an appropriate essay topic, it will probably take many drafts to produce his or her best work.

We believe the many alumni interviews Shaudi received from Harvard, Yale, Princeton, the University of Pennsylvania, and Brown, were due to his strong essay, in addition to his competitive academic standing. However, Shaudi did not end up choosing any of these East Coast schools. After all, the long essay helps a college understand a student. The short essay can help a student understand a college.

7.2. The Short, or College-Specific, Essays

Once the long essay is out of the way, the rest of the application work moves faster. Many colleges ask for a short essay along the theme of: "Why do you want to attend our college?" The purpose of this essay is so the college can tell if the student is really serious about attending, and has therefore researched the institution. Other colleges provide boxes to complete short essays in response to many short questions. The short essay or short essays may take less time than the long essay, but each short essay requires considerable attention. If the long essay is superb, for example, but the short essay is of lesser quality, it may lead an admissions officer to wonder if the student really wrote one or both of them.

As in any good writing, a short essay should contain substance to strengthen main points. The following essay is one Shaudi wrote when he applied for early decision to Stanford University. His essay is a good example for illustrating with substance (in italics).

My friends don't ask me where I want to go to college, and neither does anyone else who sees me at school. They already know. I'm known for my love of Stanford, be it from the Stanford t-shirts I don, to my Toyonomatopoeia jacket I wear almost every day, or the enthusiastic conversations with my peers. I have an insatiable curiosity for various fields of study that only Stanford can begin to satisfy. With many world-renowned schools and departments on one campus, I am free to indulge in the profound ideas that Stanford holds in store. I remember visiting my brother (now a proud Stanford alumnus) and *attending Professor Burchat's physics lecture* on time dilation. Her passionate, eloquent lecture left me hungry for the eclectic fields of study within Stanford. I want to study applied sciences in the *Nano Center*; I await the new ideas I'll encounter in Intro to Engineering; I'm eager to expand my current knowledge of the sciences; I'm curious about what to expect from comparative literature. After a week of diverse and rigorous classes, I can look forward to a Saturday *Cardinal football game* on a glorious day of California sunshine so unfamiliar in Western Washington. I especially await wearing t-shirts in the fall and on warm nights while looking at the stars without clouds to block my view. Stanford is the only place that combines academic variety and an environment that will allow my imagination to flourish. This combination is only one of many things that makes Stanford such a great place for me. After *six visits to the campus*, seeing the joy of the students at commencement and experiencing a night within a dorm, I have formed an unbreakable bond with Stanford. Four years is a long time, but if those four years are spent at Stanford, I feel it would be too short.

The weakness in this essay is a lack of focus. It broached too many aspects of the college but none was described in depth. Shaudi did not gain admission to Stanford. His essay should have showed some personal character or skill that would contribute to campus life, either academically or non-academically, rather than just receiving it from the established college community. In contrast, the next short essay, again from Tsong, is more focused. It contains not only details showing his genuine interests in and research on the University but also prospects that Tsong has high probability of joining Professor Koditscheck's research team or contributing to the Robotics laboratory.

Laws without morals are in vain. Life without passion is a bane. Throughout my life, I always value divergent thinking and problem solving skills; these values have enabled me to think critically and made many achievements possible. My values and childhood love of Legos gradually become a passion for an engineering career. I am determined to obtain a degree in mechanical engineering and apply that knowledge to build safe and effective structures that will provide society with innovative technology and more productivity. This is not only a goal, but also a passion. The Mechanical Engineering and Applied Mechanics program at Penn School of Engineering is a perfect match for me because it is my passion. During the fascinating tour of School of Engineering, I was surrounded by impressive scientific achievements: *quantum particle research, effects and functions of nanotechnology, complex robotics structures that can save a person's life,* these amazing accomplishment motivated me to excel to study hard so I can someday engage in these profound work. I am thoroughly impressed by *Professor Koditscheck's research on a bio-inspired dynamical climbing bot.* It is not only an innovative research, but also has practical applications to model behaviors of certain animal species. This is the kind of work that interests me. The Mechanical Engineering and Applied Mechanics Design and Prototyping Laboratories are the perfect place for me to obtain the essential resources to create ideas to optimize my education at Penn. I am thoroughly *excited to work with General Robotics, Automation, Sensing& Perception Laboratory* because *my experience with FIRST Robotics in high school* has proven how rewarding and fulfilling it is to engage a vibrant and collaborative environment that enhances my understanding of mechanics with other key aspects of engineering. Given the strong focus in innovation, teamwork, and research, as well as the competitive environment, University of Pennsylvania has the best programs for me to be actively engaged in research and provide me with success in my future.

A student may also tie in non-academic strength and skills with what the college may need. This strategy is well deployed in the following essay from sample student profile KCC (chapter 11), who gained early decision admission to Stanford University. It has substance. It shows research on the college. It shows how the student would contribute to campus life by joining the marching band.

When thinking of reasons as to why Stanford would be a good place for me as an undergraduate, two reasons immediately come to mind. First, I consider myself *an emerging marching band connoisseur.* As Drum Major for my high school marching band, I believe that I can discern good from bad, original from commonplace, inspiring and entertaining from nap-inducing. The Leland Stanford Junior University Marching Band is the quintessence of marching band spirit. How many other college marching bands *have award-winning records of their music*? How many other college marching bands were revived by an *under-the-table deal between band membership and current director in 1963*? How many other college marching bands *wear red blazers and fishing hats, poke fun at the treatment of the spotted owl's plight, and make giant cardboard robots*? Alas, very, very few. Second, Stanford also has the potential to finally quench my undying thirst for foreign language education. Where else can I take *Biblical Hebrew, Catalan, Igbo, Armenian, and Lakota all in one place*? Exactly. Of all the institutions of higher learning that I am applying to, Stanford's foreign language offerings are incomparable and unmatched. If given the chance to attend Stanford, I would fully utilize the foreign language resources afforded to me and bring a drive and passion hardly matched in any other academic setting.

This essay could be improved by showing more enthusiasm, not just facts. Also, it could have mentioned a specific foreign language. But, overall, this was an excellent essay.

Tip: The short essay demands research, enthusiasm, facts showing how a student can benefit a college, not vice-versa.

A "secret perk" to this marching band essay is the writer's interest in a "cold" or "less popular" major. This is an important consideration in the application process. A department with less popular majors needs students to fill seats to prevent departmental downsizing or closure. Thus, a student interested in a less popular major could have a much greater chance to be accepted in a highly selective college. This interest must be genuine. It would be unwise for a student to try to trick the admissions officer by declaring a "cold" major on the application form and then switching to a more popular major once accepted into the prestigious college. For one thing, such chicanery is easily detected by the admissions officer. For example, a science-oriented student with good transcripts and test scores in math, physics and chemistry, who claims on his application form he intends to major in a foreign language, is easily spotted as someone trying to play the system. Similarly, if a student, who had not listed any volunteer work in a church, temple or mosque, or any other humanitarian activities for that matter, claims her intended major is religious studies, this inconsistency would, again, indicate a possible ploy to trick the system.

> *Tip: Some students feign interest in a less popular major to gain admission into a larger university. This is unwise, and often easily detectable to an experienced admissions officer.*

Some people try a more subtle game. For example, in the realm of science majors, some are more popular than others. Currently, biology is the most popular science major. A science-oriented applicant could, on the college or university's application form, list an intended major in the less-popular chemical engineering program. This avoids suspicion when his or her true intention is to switch to a major in biology once admitted. This purposeful shifting within the discipline isn't necessarily the right thing to do. However, had Shaudi put chemistry, instead of biology, as his intended major in his early decision application to Stanford, he might have had a more pleasant letter.

Chapter 8. Recommendation Letters

While long and short personal essays afford students an opportunity to brag about and market themselves to admissions officers, their credibility is significantly enhanced if similar words come from someone else. Colleges and universities highly value recommendation letters from teachers, coaches, or someone who knows the student well. During our college campus visits and information sessions, we were repeatedly told that a letter written by a "famous person" such as the state governor, a senator, a Nobel laureate, or a movie star does not carry more weight than a letter from a schoolteacher. Our guides insisted the most important factor would be that the letter writer had long-term contact and a close working relationship with the student.

Intuitively, these statements make sense. A letter from a state senator, returning a favor from a family friend or a fundraiser or donor, probably won't serve a student well. Even if the student worked for the senator during a reelection campaign, it would strain believability to think the student had close contact with the senator. After all, the student would have high school classes to attend and there would be many higher-level campaign staffers between the student and the senator. As this scenario proves, it's better to stick to the basics: get letters from the high school staff.

Tip: The best – and most valued – recommendation letters come from people who worked closely enough with a student to truly get to know him or her.

Writers of these recommendation letters surely will have different writing skills. An English teacher may conceivably write a more persuasive letter than a chemistry teacher, for example. Fortunately, admissions officers take this into account, as letter writers are requested to provide their teaching areas. One thing it is hard for both admissions officers and students to know, however, is which teacher would write a student the best recommendation letter. In the classroom, some teachers are highly critical and nothing or no one is good enough for them. Other teachers may be more easygoing and easily pleased. But, the persona a teacher adopts in front of a group of students may be quite different from that teacher's feelings when writing his or her beliefs about a particular pupil. To guard against this uncertainty, a student should simply ask his or her favorite teacher to write the letter. After all, if the student likes the teacher, the teacher hopefully likes the student as well. If for no other reason, a student should cultivate a good working relationship with some teachers early in high school so the student will later have a teacher to ask to write a recommendation for college.

When asking a teacher for this favor, a student should ask early in the school year, such as in the first few weeks in September of the student's senior year. The reason is many students seek letters from popular teachers. To avoid the distraction from teaching, some schools restrict the number of letters a teacher can write each year. After all, writing recommendation letters adds extra work for teachers, in addition to their regular workload.

To further ease this burden for a teacher, a student should provide his or her recommender(s) specific information, such as a cover letter and resume. The resume should give the writer information on academic achievements, extracurricular activities, awards, and volunteer work. The cover letter should summarize the uniqueness of the student's personal traits. The cover letter should also give examples of specific interactions between the teacher and the student. Remember, a high school teacher may have hundreds of students a year. Jogging that person's memory is perfectly acceptable. Sometimes, the teacher may even quote what the student write in the cover letter to strengthen the student's case.

Tip: Early in his or her senior year, a student should ask a favorite teacher for a recommendation letter. If the teacher agrees, write examples to help remind the teacher of specific, quality interactions.

Students receive the option to reserve or to waive the right to review a recommendation letter. Most students choose to waive the right of review. It does make better sense: It shows the confidence the student entrusts in the writer. If a student simply isn't sure if a teacher would write a favorable letter, then the student should request the letter from another teacher.

Of course, a student should send a teacher who wrote a recommendation letter a thank you note after sending off the application.

Chapter 9. The Role of a Private College Counselor

Due to education budget cuts and financial strains of school districts, fewer and fewer staff have to carry more and more work. This has become the new normal in every sector of society. Consequently, high school classes are more crowded, and fewer librarians and front office staff are available to help students with an immediate issue. Even public school guidance counselors are not spared from layoffs, and, so, like teachers, those counselors remaining are typically overloaded with students. For our local high school of about 1,800 students, only five counselors are on staff. Students are assigned a counselor based on the first letter of the student's last name. Each counselor is responsible for about 360 students. One can only imagine how much face time or attention a student can get from a counselor in this situation.

Yet, the school counselor plays an important role in college applications. It is the counselor who gives out the GPA and class ranking information. It is the counselor who sends out the transcripts with the student's grades. It is the counselor who writes a third recommendation letter, which is added to the two from the teachers. So, it is in the student's best interest to see the counselor often enough that the counselor knows the student by more than the first letter of the student's last name.

> *Tip: A student should get to know his or her high school guidance counselor, often an overburdened worker who holds much responsibility and power.*

When Lauda needed a counselor's recommendation letter, he turned to his IB program counselor. She had fewer than 100 graduating students. She also was one of the original developers of the program, and, therefore, devoted much personal energy to it and her students. She had no other teaching responsibilities. She could call any student in the IB program by name in the hallway. Lauda's academic performance was top-notch, so he did receive a good recommendation letter from his counselor. But we were lucky. We did not send the counselor any information about Lauda's out-of-school activities or his volunteer work, which would have impressed the counselor more and would have helped her write an even stronger recommendation letter. Nevertheless, Lauda got into his dream college and we thought we had learned our lesson.

When Shaudi's time came for his college application, he wrote a nice cover letter and crafted a detailed resume including all his extracurricular activities and overseas trips. He even provided a list of colleges to which he intended to apply. Shaudi's first-choice teachers quickly agreed to write him recommendation letters. Then, he needed his counselor recommendation. He asked a regular counselor who advised hundreds of students, not the IB program counselor. Shaudi was not a problem student, and he had never needed advice from the counselor. So, she only knew his name through the computer screen. The counselor had a standard, three-page form for a student to complete to provide personal information so she could "get to know" the student to write a recommendation letter. Shaudi completed and returned the form and hoped for a good letter.

Once Shaudi received the rejection letter from his early decision application to Stanford University, one of his dream colleges, we realized our error. Shaudi should have asked his IB counselor to write the letter. June and I told Shaudi to ask the new IB counselor for her help. He resisted and procrastinated. He did not want to embarrass the regular counselor by asking her to withdraw her letter from The Common Application for Undergraduate College Admission at *www.commonapp.org*. Then, there was no longer enough time for the IB counselor to write the letter. Since Lauda had graduated, the IB counselor job had grown to include having to teach classes in addition to looking after the program. If Shaudi had asked that counselor for a letter sooner, or if he had visited the regular counselor in his junior year to allow her to link the name in the computer with his face, things might have turned out differently.

Clearly, when it comes to recommendation letters, deadlines are crucial. For students who are well-organized and complete tasks long before they are due, the entire college application process should go smoothly. I am sure there are many such parents with such children. But, for most high-school-age teenagers, time is a juggling act that includes school courses, homework, extracurricular activities, texting, listening to music, and checking Facebook all at the same time. Good luck to parents trying to tell their teenage student to focus on one task at a time and finish work long before the deadline so there is sufficient time for re-checks. We cannot count the number of times we tried to get Lauda and Shaudi to manage their deadlines. It always ended with unpleasant emotional tension and the "beneficial effects" lasted for minutes. It is generally known that a last-minute scramble to meet a deadline often yields a product of poor quality. However, teenagers may not believe this information. For us, our lack of credibility was compounded by a lack of firsthand information.

As foreign graduates, we did not have sufficient knowledge regarding the American college application process, nor did we know to which colleges our sons should apply, other than the big-name universities everyone in the world knows about. We had been reading books about college admission over the years. We knew the process on paper, but we lacked familiarity. I sought advice from one of my colleagues, Mark, whose child went to college the previous year. Mark had used a private college counselor for his child, and was quite happy with the fees he paid for the work. Mark said the counselor was recommended by his friend, Scott, whose child went to college two years prior. Scott, too, was happy with the fee he paid for the assistance. With our ignorance of American colleges, we thought we should find a private college counselor, too. After all, we wanted to maximize the chance of getting our children into their dream colleges. There were many private counselors available in our area; we narrowed the list down to three to interview. Whenever we buy goods or services, we consider at least three options before selecting the final one. So, we prepared a list of 10 questions and brought along our child's grades, PSAT, and SAT scores for the interview.

1. What is the scope of your service? (Do you provide only college application preparation, or do you also include high school course selection and extracurricular activity planning?)

2. Is there a limit on how many colleges your service will cover? (For example, do you only cover only five, seven, or ten college applications? Do you charge an extra fee for additional applications?)

3. What specific services do you provide for the college application? (Do you provide college selection, essay editing, preparation for a college visit or alumni interview, assistance in meeting deadlines, etc.?)

4. How do you communicate with the students? (For example, do you use email, cellphone, a face-to-face meeting, Skype? We prefer face-to-face meetings to keep pressure on a student.)

5. What is your availability? (Should we call for an appointment seven days in advance, or two days in advance, or can we usually make appointment for the same day?)

6. What time do you typically meet with the students? (For example, do you usually meet after school, on weekends, on school breaks?)

7. How many students are working with you during any given season? (We fear too many students will limit access to you, while few students may indicate a less-than-desirable service.)

8. What colleges do students with whom you worked attend?

9. What is your service fee and refund policy?

10. Is the first meeting a free consultation?

Answers from the three counselors were generic. It was hard to differentiate one from another, except by money. The service fee ran from $3,000 to $10,000 for the application process. Some began with a free consultation while others charged a $200 fee for the first hour, deductible from the total cost if we stayed with the service. There was no guarantee on acceptance to any college; thus, there was no refund after two sessions.

We made our choice based on subtle observations during the interview. We looked at the counselor's patience, mental acuity, thought process, and interaction style. For example, one of the private counselors asked to talk separately with us and with our child. The counselor asked us our expectations for our child, what his personality was like, and what our own formative years had been like. The counselor asked our student similar questions. To us, this showed the counselor was thoughtful and considerate. This move engendered our trust and locked in the agreement.

Once we chose the counselor, we made a follow-up appointment. At the second meeting, the counselor created a lengthy list of colleges that met both June's and my desires and the desires of our child. There were three groupings of schools. The first group was dream colleges, the second group was reachable colleges, and the third group was easily achievable colleges, also called "safety schools." The counselor asked our son to research and possibly visit some of the colleges. This would allow us to narrow the number of colleges for him to create applications. We credit the counselor for giving us a college list and an application plan to fit our child. The list and plan were based on high school grades, test scores, and the counselor's experience of acceptance rates at various colleges.

Our child spent subsequent meetings with the counselor planning his long essay. Sometimes, this was frustrating for us, as parents. Our private counselor did not say anything negative about Lauda's or Shaudi's long essays, despite our concern the essays were premature and no progress was being made, in spite of multiple meetings with the counselor throughout the summer between each child's junior and senior year. Once the fall term started for senior year, we knew spare time would become a precious commodity. At times, June and I felt the weeks were slipping away. Each version of the essay would improve by only a few words. By the time the summer ended, the essay would be through several revisions, but, then, with the pressures of the senior high school year starting, essay progress would become even slower.

But, unlike parents, private counselors have professional standards: required hours of continuing education, attendance at annual private counselor conferences, and a certain number of college campus visits. They have a standard code of conduct; they cannot write the essay for the students but can only provide guidance and suggestions on topic selection, simple grammar, and spelling. June and I gradually started to appreciate the role of the private counselor, which is to keep the application rolling and meet the deadlines, not to do the work for the students. A student's writing should be a reflection of his or her own ability. This is fair. Any other expectations beyond these for the private counselor would be unreasonable. Our initial frustration was because we felt our sons had the capability to achieve better, but they needed inspiration to fire their ambition and motivation. In hoping for a motivational service, we didn't realize we were expecting something akin to a private, personal coach like one employed by a royal family for grooming an heir. We learned our lesson: The counselor does a parent's job in a more acceptable way, consistently pushing the students to meet deadlines.

Tip: If the family can afford it, a private college counselor can help enforce deadlines and gently push students in ways a parent sometimes cannot.

Later, when friends asked us how we felt about working with a private college counselor and whether the cost was worthwhile, we explained how a counselor cannot guarantee a college acceptance, nor can the counselor do work for a student. However, a parent who is tired of nagging a child cannot discount the benefit of a counselor keeping an application moving and meeting deadlines without a last-minute rush. A public school counselor will not be able to do this; a parent has to worry about hostile feelings from a temperamental teenager. So, a private counselor who charges a high fee might not be worthwhile, particularly for a family with financial strains. Also, a student with a good time management skills, an inner drive to achieve great things, and an organized nature would do well in the college application process without external pressure or assistance. For our very different sons, we now believe Lauda would have gotten into his first choice college without the guidance of a private college counselor. By contrast, Shaudi did not get into his early decision college despite help from a private college counselor. We used the same counselor twice and would probably use her again if we had a third child. Why? Do we have too much money and don't know what to do with it? No. We still have a 1996 Toyota Corolla (as of 2012), and I drove it to work every day despite my six-digit salary until Lauda got his driver's license. But, when it comes to our children's education and well-being, we want to maximize any element that could exert even the slightest positive influence toward a favorable outcome.

When we surveyed Lauda and Shaudi after they were in college about their opinion and feelings toward private college counseling, they confirmed what we believed: "Because I had to meet with her, I had to complete the assignments from her," Lauda said. "She kept me on time before the deadlines," Shaudi added. To us, this feedback reinforces the need for a face-to-face communication with a counselor (not Skype, email, phone, text or other detached exchanges). This "remote control" would defeat the purpose of hiring a private counselor.

Chapter 10. Which College to Visit or Apply to?

When June and I were in China during our college years, we only heard about a handful of colleges or universities in other countries. Once I entered my graduate research, I learned more names of foreign universities, as these institutions play major roles in scientific discovery. The bigger the university, the more likely it has more research publications in circulation. But, as research topics get deeper and narrower at the doctoral and postdoctoral level, publication sources become limited to just a few research laboratories.

So, when June and I came to the United States, we were familiar with some big-name universities. Once we lived in the country for a few years, we learned more university names, this time via intercollegiate sports. By the time Lauda was looking at colleges and our private college counselor produced the three lists for us to consider and prioritize, we picked college names we recognized and crossed off those we hadn't heard of. In truth, we did not know much about individual university strength or quality. We did double-check each university's status on the annual ranking from *US News & World Report.* However, neither our counselor nor other education experts gave this list much credit[7]. Still, June and I equated a university's fame to the educational quality it would provide. Name recognition meant excellence to us. In preserving only schools we "knew" on the dream group, reachable group, and safety group, June and I were writing ourselves a prescription for parental psychological satisfaction, not considering whether our child would fit in to a certain college or thrive at a particular university. We never considered whether the strength of a college met the interests of our student.

One thing we had considered, though, was aesthetics. Our family vacations during Lauda and Shaudi's growing-up years were typically driving excursions. We would camp in a State or National Park in the suburbs for the night, enjoy the parks, and then venture into the city for groceries and sightseeing during the day. Most cities held a college campus. Initially, both June and I were disappointed at these campus visits. To us, the big name universities should have exuded something so impressive that we would want to bend our knees to kiss the ground in an atmosphere so solemn we would hold our breath. This did not happen. We looked for a grandiose gate like the ones back in China that would signal our arrival to the entrance of the campus. We looked for the otherworldly walls that would encircle the space that held such academic fame, such fertile minds, such distinguished accomplishments. We didn't see gates. We didn't see walls. But, these must be exceptions, we thought. So, we kept visiting college campuses. Eventually, we were pleased by a handful of universities with British-style architecture and layout, but the vast majority of the college campuses were disappointing.

In time, we stopped vacationing in college towns. June and I also paused to reassess our thoughts. We wondered what made these un-gated, non-walled US colleges and universities such powerhouses of intellectual discovery. It must be the "disappointing" openness of these colleges without walls, June and I decided. The boundary-less campus signals the freedom to move, implies the philosophy of a free-thinking education, reflects a frameless teaching style, encourages the adventurous mind into unknown fields, and promotes the spirit to challenge conventional wisdom. Having gained appreciation for the old saying "looks can be deceiving," June and I decided we should discount a college or university's appearance.

But, as Lauda approached his application deadlines, we still debated.

"Do we really need to visit the campus?" I asked June. "We can go and look at it once acceptance letters are in hand. After all, we'll send Lauda regardless of our feelings about the campus if one of his top five colleges sends us a letter of admission."

June countered, "Since a visit to the college is a tradition, let's try it."

With a narrowed-down list of colleges to work from, I took Lauda on several of my trips to medical conferences on the East Coast. We would take a rental car to see two college campuses in one day. Every college website offers a calendar of group campus tours. It's a good idea to sign up online, weeks before a visit, so the parent and student can see the campus at a favored time and day. Also, it's important to secure a spot in case the group becomes too large to allow drop ins.

Tip: A few weeks before a campus visit, sign up online
for a group tour. A reservation ensures a preview of
the school at a preferred time, on a preferred day.

These tours typically last two hours. During the first hour, an admissions officer will usually lead an informational presentation and Q&A session. During the second hour, a student will usually lead a campus tour showing eateries, residence halls, classrooms, libraries, and occasionally, laboratories, and other amenities.

Good questions to ask during the information session include: "What kind of students are you looking for?" "What scores or grades do you expect?" "What did students in your last graduating class go on to do?" "How can a student get accepted into your college?" "How can a student get financial aid or paid work? "What is the average class size?"

Good questions to ask during the tour include: "Do most freshmen live on campus?" "How difficult is it to get into coveted classes?" "Do students need a car?" "Have you been mostly pleased by the challenge of your coursework?" "How difficult is it to get an appointment with a professor or an academic advisor?" "Why are you pleased with this university?"

I quickly realized these organized campus visits were much more enlightening and informative than the ones we did by ourselves a few years ago. They also accomplished two other important purposes: First, they helped motivate our high school student to work harder to achieve entrance to an impressive university. Second, they informed the admissions office our student was interested enough in the college to make the effort and encumber the expense to be there, and if accepted, would be more likely to attend the college than someone who never made the trip. This is a significant assurance for an admissions officer. If a student is not likely to attend the college if offered admission, why bother to accept the student? After all, if the student does not enroll after receiving an acceptance letter, enrollment rate statistics will suffer in college rankings from *US News & World Report*.

Tip: A campus visit can motivate a student, and the student's name in the tour log can assure an admissions officer of the student's intention to enroll.

Some people believe colleges are changing their tactics as they become more mindful of these statistics that can form public opinion. Accepting fewer students, but wait-listing more students, forces up a college or university's enrollment rate (the number of students who accept an offer to enroll divided by the number of acceptance letters sent out). Yet, the college or university can still fill the incoming class, if needed, from the waitlist pool. Based on enrollment rates from previous years, the number of acceptance letters sent could be 30% to 80% more than the actual number of spots available in the class. For example, a popular college may actually have 1,500 spots but will send out 2,000 acceptance letters, gambling 500 students will not enroll. This yields a 75% enrollment rate, considered excellent by the rating magazines. For the equal number of spots in its upcoming class, a less desirable college may have to send out 4,500 acceptance letters. This yields a 33% enroll rate, considered mediocre by the rating agencies. I do not have hard data to back up this theoretical speculation but it makes intuitive sense.

At every college campus Lauda and I visited, I had a notebook ready at all the sessions. I took copious notes from discussions led by admissions officials and by student guides. Lauda just listened. He wrote nothing down. I was not quite sure what Lauda took in from those college tours. Was it necessary or worthwhile to embark on them? June and I weren't sure until it was time to work on Lauda's actual college applications. Then, Lauda explained he did not want to apply to some of the colleges he visited, although June and I would have liked him to do so. He also resisted the idea of applying to a college he had not visited. Lauda wanted to apply to the private colleges where there were only 20 to 30 families in each tour group. He did not want to apply to the larger, public colleges where there were 50 to 100 families in each tour group. We had not anticipated this reaction. But, we had to proceed his way.

In contrast, for Shaudi, we only visited campuses on the West Coast. We did offer him the opportunity to visit colleges on the East Coast, but he declined due to his busy school schedule. As before, we signed up online for a tour date and time, and signed in again on the day of the information session. Again, as parents, we took more notes than our student did. To our surprise, however, and contrary to Lauda, Shaudi preferred the larger, busier and crowded colleges. He also did not mind applying to colleges he had not visited.

Both our sons, it turned out, had learned something on their college tours. Both learned what type of place he would feel at home, once he left our house to attend college.

> *Tip: On campus tours, a parent may have specific concerns,*
> *such as classes and programs. A student, by contrast, may*
> *soak up the general atmosphere, intuitively trying to figure*
> *out if this type of school best fits his or her personality.*

When the final tally was in, Shaudi did have a much higher acceptance rate among the colleges he visited as compared to those he had not. Perhaps it was a matchmaking experience: Having visited a place, Shaudi instinctively knew if he would enjoy learning there, while the admissions officer could recognize the harmony of campus to student via the application materials. Or, perhaps showing interest in the college by paying a visit to campus played a role in the acceptance decision. The following data may be worth pondering.

Lauda visited or applied to 15 universities:

College	Visited	Applied	Accepted
Brown University	yes	no	no
Columbia University	yes	yes	no
Harvard University	yes	no	no
MIT	yes	yes	no
Northwestern University	yes	yes	yes
Pomona College	yes	yes	yes
Stanford University	yes	yes	yes
UC-Berkeley	yes	no	no
UC-Los Angeles	yes	no	no
University of Chicago	yes	yes	yes
University of Pennsylvania	yes	yes	yes

U of Southern California	yes	yes	yes
University of Washington-Honor	yes	yes	yes
Yale University	yes	yes	no
Washington U at St. Louis	no	yes	yes

Here the acceptance rate among the visited and applied to colleges is 66.7% or 6/9. Since Lauda only applied to one college that he did not visit and yet got an acceptance, the number is too much a random chance for statistical reasoning.

Shaudi visited or applied to 16 universities:

College	Visited	Applied	Accepted
Brown University	no	yes	no
Columbia University	no	yes	no
Connell University	no	yes	yes
Harvard University	no	yes	no
Northwestern University	no	yes	no
Pomona College	yes	yes	yes
Princeton University	no	yes	no
Stanford University	yes	yes	no
UC-Berkeley	yes	no	no
UC-Los Angeles	yes	no	no
University of Chicago	no	yes	no
University of Pennsylvania	no	yes	no

U of Southern California	yes	yes	yes
University of Washington-- Honor	yes	yes	yes
Yale University	no	yes	no
Washington U at St. Louis	no	yes	no

Here the statistics become more intriguing as there is data on both sides of the story: the acceptance rate among the visited and applied to colleges is 75% or ¾ whilst the acceptance rate among the not-visited but applied to colleges is 10% or 1/10.

Of the 17 separate colleges one of our sons applied to, we visited 14, and to some many times. We were fortunate; our private college advisor helped us prioritize where to make our visits and send our applications. For a student without the assistance of a private college counselor, however, it is easy enough to compile a list of colleges to visit or apply to. To generate the three lists our advisor created – dream colleges (low probability to get in), reachable colleges (good probability to get in) and safety net colleges (high probability to get in) – college guides and reference books can help. To avoid purchasing these books, it is worth checking the public library and high school library for copies. We used mostly the *Fiske College Guide*[8] and *Princeton College Review*[9], and occasionally cross-referenced *The Ultimate College Guide by US News & World Report*[10]. These books summarize more than 400 four-year colleges and universities. They also include statistics for the current student body, as well as the SAT scores, GPAs and high school class rank of admitted students in previous years. The books also describe costs, admission requirements, and the faculty to student ratio.

Armed with this data, a parent or student could compare high school grades and scores to see which college might be in the dream, reachable, and safety net categories. Then, look at the acceptance rate. Highly selective colleges have a rate of 5-15%. Public state universities may have a 30-50% acceptance rate. Armed with this knowledge of their "enemy" and their "army," a parent and student can have a good chance of "winning the war." However, as mentioned in previous chapters, the college admissions process has a subjective component. A student who fears low probability for getting into a dream college may still have a chance. Conversely a student who is surely a shoo-in at a safety net college could be surprised by a rejection letter. The best strategy is to apply to more than one college in each group.

Tip: The statistics in college reference books and guides can help determine what tier a college is for a student: dream, reachable, or safety net. Apply to more than one of each.

But should a family also invest in visiting college campuses?

When asked about the role the college campus visit played in their college application process, neither Lauda nor Shaudi could offer a firm positive or negative feeling. However, as parents not educated in this country and unfamiliar with the US college system, June and I felt it was a useful exercise, and it provided us some basic knowledge to help our children. We liked to be involved in our children's developmental events and life milestones. These visits also gave us some relief and lifelong good memories that we, as parents, did our best in raising our sons and we fulfilled our responsibilities to the best of our abilities. So, if time and money allow, it is better to sign up and go for the campus tour to assure yourselves … and the admission officers..

Chapter 11. Final Packaging and Sample Student Profiles

It had been a hectic six months for Lauda. He was working on the pieces required for his college applications: exams, academics, essays, extracurriculars. Frankly, it was the most stressful period in his entire school career. But, the light was starting to become visible at the end of the tunnel. In December of his high school senior year, we helped him carefully assemble all the pieces into a complete package. Back then, it was still a paper application. I used an old typewriter to fill in demographics and other hard data on the form. (Lauda's handwriting would have made the admissions office dizzy.) Lauda printed, cut, fitted, and pasted his essays in the spaces provided. He then photocopied the pages and signed the final form. Lauda's teachers had already sent their recommendation letters directly to the colleges. His sealed transcript lay in a smaller envelope to be inserted into the larger, brown envelope. June carried the parcel to the post office. She sent it by Express Mail with a tracking number for security.

In some ways, the old method was more helpful to the student. On any college application form, a student must be careful and reasonable when deciding, for example, how many extracurricular activities to include. On paper, with limited space to write, it was easy to see when there was too much information. After all, sporadic activities may not support the main theme. An illustration of this idea would be the student who is strong in science with many awards from competitions. This student should include participation in science-related volunteer work, but probably should not mention charitable lawn mowing for elderly neighbors. Such off-topic information could dilute the strength of the applicant and distract the university reviewers.

By the time Shaudi was applying to colleges and universities, everything was online using the common application form. Before clicking the submit button, we had a second set of eyes double check the forms to ensure information was correct and relevant. We also printed the pages to ensure every word was within the page borders, as admission officers would be reading the application and making their decision based on printed versions of the forms.

> *Tip: Printing application forms helps students see their information the same way admissions officers will eventually read it.*

For both our sons, we started peering at these application forms, on paper or online, as our neighbors were setting up and then taking down their Christmas decorations. That is because both our sons applied to college early. The deadline to apply for early action or early decision varies among colleges, usually from December 1 to January 1. A student may only apply to one college during this "early" period. For colleges accepting Early Action applications, a student does not need to commit to the college if accepted and can still apply to other colleges during the regular application period. But for colleges offering Early Decision, a student is locked into the college if accepted and cannot apply to any others. Violation of this contract could have serious consequences, ruining the student's college dream. More and more colleges are offering early decision because it assures the college accepted students will enroll.

Whether it's early action or early decision, the acceptance rate from the "early" applicant pool is much higher than the regular pool, in the range of 30-50%. Some colleges admit more than half their incoming class in this way. Therefore, fewer spots are left for applicants in the regular decision pool, which has a correspondingly lower acceptance rate, in the range of 5-9% for highly desirable colleges. If a student did not get accepted during the early application period, it is likely to be more difficult to get into a highly selective college.

> *Tip: It can be easier to earn acceptance to a competitive university by strategically and ethically using early action or early decision applications.*

After sending in the early action or early decision application, neither student nor parent can relax. Ideally, the student will receive an acceptance notification. However, the student should still work on short essays required by other colleges. If the student is rejected by the early school, the student must therefore apply to other schools. If the essays are already complete, the student can finish the other applications more quickly.

However, rejection or acceptance are not the only two results of early action or early decision. A "deferred" letter is the third possibility. If a student is deferred, it means the college or university will place the student's application in the regular decision pool. The admissions office will reconsider the application once it receives the next wave of regular applicants. A deferred student should still apply to other colleges or universities, just in case the preferred institution does not grant admission.

> *Tip: Instead of relaxing, early applicants should continue to draft short essays for other schools.*

It can be difficult to imagine how a student application package and profile should appear. The following are sample student application packages and profiles. These are real cases. The students are all 2011 graduates from our local high school, where Lauda and Shaudi graduated. The students gave their consent to use their information in this book, but their full names are withheld to protect their privacy. The information is not altered or revised, even to correct for typographical or grammatical errors.

Student CDA Profile:

Statistics:

Class Rank: 32 weighted; 48 unweighted;   Class Size: 579
GPA: 3.91 (at time of application)
SAT I: Best total: 2240   (700R, 800W, 740M)
SAT II: Math 2c: 800   Physics: 700
IB/AP: IB Film SL 6

Honors and Awards:

1.   State Solo/Ensemble Finalist on Cello (9th grade).
2.   Northwest Chopin Festival Piano Honorable Mention (9-11th grade).
3.   National Music Teacher Association Piano finalist (9-11th grade).
4.   WJEA (state journalism) sports feature writing finalist (11th grade).
5.   JEA (nationals) broadcast news writing honorable mention (11th grade).
6.   IBWSC (IB World Student Conference) North America delegate.
7.   Principal's Athletic Award (11th and 12th grade)

Extracurricular Activities:

1.   Varsity tennis (11-12th grade) 15 hrs/wk; 12 wks/yr
2.   Senior Class Secretary (12th grade) 3 hrs/wk; 35 wks/yr
3.   Cello (9-12th grade) 8 hrs/wk; 50wks/yr
4.   Piano (9-12th grade) 4 hrs/wk; 50wks/yr
5.   Newspaper Staff sports editor (11th grade), features editor (12th grade), 7 hrs/wk; 35wks/yr
6.   Honor Society Vice President (12th grade) 2 hrs/wk; 15wks/yr
7.   Varsity Track and Field (9-11th grade) 15 hrs/wk; 10wks/yr
8.   TIP (Total Immersion Program) English tutor at Beida University (summer before 11th grade) 40 hrs/wk; 3wks/yr
9.   Kiwanis Key Club service member (10-12th grade) 2 hrs/wk; 20wks/yr

The Long Essay:
Common App: Evaluate a significant experience, achievement, risk you have taken, or ethical dilemma you have faced and its impact on you. WC: 739

In the spring of 2010, I was selected as an ambassador to represent my high school at the first IB World Student Conference (IBWSC) ever held in the U.S. The conference, which took place from August 8 to 14 on Oregon State

University's campus, welcomed 280 students from 12 countries from as far as Japan and Venezuela. The mission statement aimed to foster within each IB student, the central goal of the international IB community: "Sharing our Humanity." The conference covered six international topics: global poverty, infectious disease, peacekeeping, education, environmental concerns, and technological divide. My exposure to the variety of global concerns addressed widened my perception of the world and enlightened me to the various ways we, as global citizens, can act to address these issues.

My participation in the IBWSC expanded my understanding of the situations of struggling countries throughout the world and empowered me to take initiative as a young member in society, to galvanize cultural awareness and global communication. A keynote presentation by Peace One Day creator Jeremy Gilley resonated with my newly developed perspective to global citizenship, in which he delineated the various methods high school students can use to influence their communities. Near the end of the conference, I decided that events such as a school awareness day, community fundraiser, or even organized soccer tournament geared toward promoting peace could benefit my local community. I reached the epiphany that these events would foster in students a sense of hope and progress in contributing to the international humanitarian sector.

At the conference, students were split into groups of twenty with the goal of creating an IB CAS service project for implementation at local school and community levels. My group created the organization Hands Full of Hope, with the intent of bettering a variety of causes rather than supporting a single one. We considered the conference's six international issues and united under the idea that due to our varied interests, it would be most beneficial to fundraise under a campaign aimed to encompass all of these problems.

One of the most important opportunities provided by the IBWSC was the chance to live with and better understand the lifestyles and personalities of various individuals from around the world. This exposure to cultural diversity helped me to acquire a better sense of other teenagers' lives as affected by their social norms and customs back home. One friend I made from Venezuela, Kevin, left an irrevocable personal account on me. Kevin and I had many things in common from hobbies, to family background, to even taste in music. However, the one major difference between us was in the area of our two countries' political systems. The system of Venezuela limited Kevin's sense of security in his neighborhood and ability to speak out at school. He complained of the strictness of government control as well as the lack of organized police forces in his community. Drug deals, gang fights and raids were common and his neighborhood is not safe. Kevin cannot leave his house carrying a phone or wearing a nice shirt because he would be stopped and it would be taken. Situations are so dangerous that his parents had nearly been shot while attempting to prevent the raid of a neighbor's house. I on the other hand, have lived the majority of my life in a middle-class suburban neighborhood in Washington, without ever having experienced such discomforts.

Considering the litany of anguish and frustration-filled events Kevin described, I began to consider my future plans in a broader context, recognizing the various inadequacies throughout the world that need to be addressed. Since that day, I knew I would never turn my back on helping fight against a global issue, acknowledging that I could very much well be giving up on a friend in need.

The IBWSC has broadened my outlook on the global perspective of cultural and international problems. The personal stories I heard from other youths around the world of how political disarray, global poverty, illness and other problems have affected their lives were incredibly moving. I was jolted to the immediacy and magnitude of these issues and now understand how important it is for me to help counter these problems. With this new realization in mind, I strive each day to improve in my walk of global citizenship, to reach out with a kind heart and helping hand to my fellow citizens of our shared planet earth.

The Short Essay (for Northwestern University)
Why do you think this college is a good fit for you.

I believe NU's Communications school can provide me the ideal preparation for a career in dentistry and develop leadership abilities to further my influence in global outreach programs. As an undergraduate, I plan to major in Communications, apply to dental school after receiving my Bachelor's, while pursuing a minor in music along the way. I believe Northwestern University's diverse community offers a host of opportunities that will complement my various passions, ranging from non-major secondary interests in music and creative writing to major-related humanitarianism involvements. NU's dynamic environment appeals to me because I can simultaneously involve myself in many different sectors of student life, without having to sacrifice academic performance. The School of Communication, cello and newspaper writing are several of the opportunities available at Northwestern that I would like to pursue.

I am interested in the School of Communication, particularly the Department of Communication Studies, because of the curriculum's focused agenda regarding the social and cultural aspects of human interaction. As an aspiring member of global humanitarianism, I am cognizant to the benefits of being culturally literate and having the 'soft' communication and interpersonal skills that will enable a smooth transition to the work place. I have been interested in dentistry for many years because of the strong impression my dentist made on me. During a routine oral checkup, my dentist spotted an unusual lump in the mouth of one of her patients, which led to quick treatment for possible oral cancer. Because of the detection, she was able to save the patient's life, an act of heroism that inspired me to pursue dentistry, as a means to promote oral healthcare around the world. After dental school, I plan to participate in the Doctors Without Borders program, where I can share dental healthcare in countries which otherwise would lack it.

NU's Department of Music has a strong reputation for producing talented musicians and offers a wide range of undergraduate opportunities. Playing cello is my favorite hobby and an activity I do not want to give up in college. As a music minor, the Department of Music provides private cello instruction so I may further my cello education while simultaneously pursuing other interests. I plan to take advantage of NU's Philharmonia, one of many opportunities available to non-major musicians on campus, which can provide me with an excellent source for advancing both my orchestral musicianship and personal cello technique.

Since my junior year in high school, I have been an editor of the school newspaper. I have grown fond of both creative and investigative news writing and want to further develop my journalistic writing skills in college. When I talked with several Northwestern students about the opportunities available to undergraduates on campus, I was pointed to Northwestern's independent student-run newspaper, *The Daily Northwestern* and the student-run satirical news source, the *Northwestern Flipside*. I have not decided which publication to participate in as I am interested in both classic and satirical news writing. However, for both papers, I was told I do not have to be a member on staff to contribute and could submit my works as a freelance writer. Writing for either paper would be an excellent opportunity to offer my viewpoints to Northwestern and contribute to the dynamic community. Freelance writing would be most suitable for me because of the multitude of activities I would like to pursue in college. Northwestern's vibrant community with a focused ideology on academic excellence would provide me with an environment conducive for shaping me into an active, community-minded individual.

Colleges granted an alumni interview:

1. Cornell University
2. Duke University
3. Northwestern University
4. University of Pennsylvania
5. University of Southern California (merit-scholarship on-campus interview)

Colleges granted acceptance letter:

1. Northwestern University

2. University of Southern California
3. University of Michigan
4. University of Washington

Colleges granted wait list:

1. Cornell University
2. Washington University in St. Louis

College selected to attend:

1. Northwestern University

Student JJB Profile:

Statistics:

Class Rank: 8 weighted; 24 un-weighted   Class Size: 579
GPA: 3.964 (at time of application)
SAT I:Best total: 2240   (710R, 730W, 800M)
SAT II: Math 2c: 750   Chem: 770   Bio: 760
IB/AP: IB Chem SL 7   IB Spanish SL 6

Honors and Awards:

1. Co-Captain HS Varsity Tennis team (12th grade)
2. WIAA Outstanding Scholastic Award
3. Washington Scholar Award
4. National Honor (&Junior) Society Certificate of Membership
5. Northshore School District Junior High Championship 1st Place

Extracurricular Activities:

1. HS Varsity Tennis team (9th, 10th, 11th, 12th grade). 20h/w, 15w/y
2. Viola at Seattle Youth Symphony Orchestra (9th, 10th, 11th grade). 10h/w, 40w/y
3. Charity volunteer medical care in rural China (8th-12th grade). 40/w, 2w/y.
4. Nurse assistant and research assistant (9th-12th grade). 3h/w, 12w/y.
5. Sponsor and participant: Relay for Life for American cancer society (9th-12th grade). 24h/w, 1w/y.
6. Key Club (10th-12th grade). 1h/w, 40w/y
7. BioQuest Academy Summer internship (12th grade). 30/w,2w/y.
8. Johns Hopkins Talented Youth summer program (10th,11th). 107h/w,3w/y.

119

9. Linker Crew Leader (10th,11th). 1h/w,40w/y.
10. Science Olympiad club (11th,12th). 1h/w,40w/y.
11. Independent Tutor (11th,12th). 1h/w, 40w/y.
12. Book Keeper for Intellectual Consulting and Exchange LLC (9th-12th). 1h/w, 40w/y.

The Long Essay

Evaluate a significant experience, achievement, risk you have taken, or ethical dilemma you have faced and its impact on you.

140...160...180mmHg. I stopped squeezing the pump and carefully turned the metal wheel between my thumb and forefinger, listening intently over the whistle of air as the needle wound down to 0. I repeated the process again. 140, 160, 180...0. Couldn't get it. Again: 140, 160, 180...0. Still nothing. Why couldn't I get this patient's blood pressure? I was puzzled.

For every summer since the 8th grade, I have returned to China as part of a small medical team led by my father. We provide free, basic medical care for the rural villages of Baofeng in the Henan province where he spent his childhood and many of our relatives still reside. Having observed the villagers' poor health and limited access to care during my childhood visits there, I was aware of the great need for this service. Naturally, I was eager to become part of the team to aid the people as much as I could.

During my first trip, we spent 25 continuous hours traveling; after landing in Beijing from a 12-hour flight, we took a 13-hour train ride to Baofeng. Since the train's sleeper-tickets were sold-out we had to buy seat-tickets for the ride. Even with sleep deprivation from the plane trip, dozing off was a challenge made more difficult by the noxious fumes of smokers and uncomfortable seats. Despite these conditions, my situation was still quite "luxurious". I saw rows of passengers who could afford neither bed nor sitting ticket and instead endured an overnight trip standing. What caught my attention was how complacent they appeared which made me see how fortunate I was, but in a few hours I would see many more that were even less fortunate.

Upon arriving, we immediately went to our respective tasks. One team traveled to the local, poorly-supported hospitals to discuss diabetes awareness while I stayed with the other team at the de facto clinic we set up in a communal area near my grandmother's hut. Soon, a line of patients snaked through the muddy corridors of the village as we performed blood pressure and glucose tests on countless villagers. Thus started my two-week health mission.

Every day consisted of seven hours of testing over one hundred patients. My ears continuously throbbed with pain from the stethoscope, but for each patient I put it back on. My discomfort paled in comparison to the hardships that these villagers experienced on a daily basis. For many, this was the first check-up of their lifetime, and for some, they would find out they were diabetic or hypertensive despite never having heard these words before.

140, 160, 180...0mmHg. As the summer sun blazed above and sweat dripped down my cheeks, my left hand robotically wiped the perspiration while my right continued to pump the sphygmomanometer. I listened for an initial beat but instead received a barrage of beats that ceased as quickly as they had started. No matter how many times I repeated the process, I kept on hearing this barrage of beats. Confused, I consulted a team member, a Registered Nurse. She discovered that my inability to get a reading was caused by the patient's extreme blood pressure, 220/140, that was beyond the limit for which I had been testing. This signaled a hypertensive emergency, so the patient was immediately given medications that we had brought with us. The patient came back the next day for reexamination: 140/90. The team physician patted me on the back for my perseverance in preventing "a potentially life threatening stroke". It was then that I understood the reality and seriousness of what I was doing.

I remember feeling my patients' hands calloused from working in the fields, hardened to the extent that I could barely prick their fingers to draw blood for testing. I vividly recall another incident two summers ago in which a patient who was paralyzed from a stroke was brought in on a homemade wheelchair made from knotted bamboo and wheels taken from a wagon. Her eyes were dim and void of spirit, her face just as lifeless. The family eagerly looked at us, waiting for a cure to her ailment. I had no idea of how to say 'stroke' or 'thrombolytic therapy' in Chinese, and my partners had no way of communication other than through me. I had thought that my CPR certification and glucose test training would prepare me sufficiently for this trip. I was clearly wrong; they were looking for something that I could not give them. Wanting to do the most I could, I tested her glucose level which came out to be very low. We told the family to feed her some candy when they got home, and our physician would contact them to prescribe a medication regiment. They came later that day for re-examination; her eyes had an unseen brightness and her face, a livelier expression. The family showered us with thanks, offering to treat us to dinner (the highest local social honor) despite financial hardship. I thought that we didn't really do much for the patient because her limbs were still paralyzed, but the family did not feel the same way. They praised us for bringing life back into her, convincing me that small things really can make a difference. Standing there, I felt that I had sincerely made an impact, a feeling with which I had been unfamiliar before taking part in this annual medical trip.

Our time in the village eventually came to a close. Much like the eyes of my patient, I, too, had changed. Each time, I entered China not knowing what to expect but left enriched by the experiences accumulated from my many trips. No longer a passive bystander, I took a more active role, and I now truly understand the need for this service having seen the condition of the villagers and personally being touched by them. Holding the hundreds of hands hardened by hours of commitment to land and home, my appreciation for the contributions of my fellow human beings grew immensely. As a caregiver, I've been shown by my patients that we are all uniquely valuable. Each summer, I eagerly look to return to Baofeng because I know that I can make a difference in other people's lives. However, I always keep in mind that the true reason for my actions comes from the fact that there is still much to be done.

The Short Essay (for Pomona College)

This past summer, I was fortunate enough to have had the chance to attend BioQuest Academy, a two week lab technician job-shadowing and educational program sponsored by the Seattle Biomedical Research Institute (SBRI), which is known as a world class infectious disease research institute. As part of the curriculum, I was exposed to many unfamiliar and daunting facts that have been hidden from me for most my life. For example, the catastrophic effects of malaria on the people in Africa, the deaths around the world caused by AIDS and the stigma it creates, the vulnerability of children with tuberculosis, and the need and difficulty of finding vaccines for such malignant diseases. Something I found very engaging was seeing how the things learned in a classroom are actually applied in a real life setting. While my knowledge that cytosine binds with guanine in the DNA seems to lack a clear application in the real world, I eventually learned to recognize how the comparison of these unique sequences among species of female anopheles mosquitoes provides the fundamental basis for a malaria vaccine. This made me aware that some of the things I learn in school that may seem pointless actually do have some worth. Beyond the intellectual enlightenment of my classroom knowledge, I was taught many technical skills that the scientists at SBRI use to develop vaccines. Some of these techniques include nanodropping, sequence analyzing, and gel electrophoresis, ones that I could never have the opportunity to learn in a high school setting. It is exciting to know that the invaluable information provided by these methods can potentially provide a cure or treatment for some of the world's deadliest diseases. I have developed a real sense of responsibility and clear purpose of learning from this experience and at Pomona I hope to incorporate this newfound set of values. Though I may not pursue this specific career pathway, whatever ambitions I will partake will employ what I took in from this valuable experience. My choices, be it the classes I take to the organizations or groups I affiliate myself with, will be influenced by my knowledge of the importance of helping a global effort and working for the greater good. Even if I pursue a career not involving the physical skills I learned at Bioquest, I will still find a way to make a beneficial impact on the global scene. The work that I hope to do at Pomona will not be just for a good grade or to impress teachers but for a long term goal, for solving real life issues and helping a global effort.

Colleges granted an alumni interview:

1. Brown University
2. Harvard University
3. Princeton University
4. University of Pennsylvania
5. Yale University

Colleges granted acceptance letter:

1. Cornell University
2. Pomona College
3. University of Southern California
4. University of Washington Honor Program

Colleges granted wait list:

1. Brown University
2. Northwestern University
3. Washington University at St Louis
4. University of Chicago

College selected to attend:

1. Pomona College

Student KCC Profile:

Statistics:

Class Rank: 19 weighted; 11 unweighted   Class Size: 579
GPA: 3.98 (at time of application)
SAT I:Best total: 1900   (690R, 700W, 690M)
ACT: English: 32; Math: 34; Reading: 34; Science: 36
IB/AP: IB Philosophy SL 6

<u>Honors and Awards:</u>

1. Honor Roll (9, 10, 11 grades)
2. September Club Member of the Month (12th grade)

<u>Extracurricular Activities:</u>

1. Tap dancer at Woodinville Dance Academy/Premiere Dance Center/PDC Competition Team; 6 hrs wk, 45 wks a year
2. Drum Major for Inglemoor High School Marching Band and Pep Band; 6 hrs/wk, 13 wks/yr
3. Inglemoor High School Symphonic Band and Wind Ensemble; 4 hrs/wk, 28 wks/yr
4. Organized food items at Hopelink (stocked produce, interfaced with clients, etc.); 3 hrs/wk, 25 wks/year
5. Prom Planning Committee 2011; 2 hrs/wk, 38 wks/yr
6. Vice President of IHS Model UN (junior and senior year); 1 hr/wk, 38 wk/yr
7. Principal Dancer (2009-2010) and Tap Teacher (2010-2011) for IHS Musical "Beauty and the Beast" (2010) and "Thoroughly Modern Millie" (2011); 6 hrs/wk, 12 wks/yr
8. JV Track and Field (junior year); 10 hrs/wk, 12 wks/yr
9. Self-employed tap dance and drum set teacher; 2 hr/wk, 40 wks/yr
10. LINK Crew Leader; 7 hrs/wk, 3 wks/yr

<u>The Long Essay:</u>
Evaluate a significant experience, achievement, risk you have taken, or ethical dilemma you have faced and its impact on you.

I love food. I have always loved food. I've grown my own food, I've taken food classes, and I've even written research papers and critical analyses on food. Food and me, we go hand in hand. There's something unexplainable in the feeling you get when you eat an absolutely angelic piece of pizza, a beautifully crafted tomato strata, or magnificent, steaming paella. A visceral reaction is had, something so primitive in its history, but advanced in its scope. Food is something to have a relationship with, not just something to fulfill an appetite. Yet, food is becoming sterilized. Not in a literal sense of pasteurization, but in the sense that our food is becoming disconnected from being a vital asset to American culture. People do not know where their food comes from, what their food contains, or how healthy it is for them or the earth. Therein lays the problem. In order to combat this apathy towards the sources of our food, we must focus on the local and the homegrown so as to create a food culture that is healthy in both mind and body.

Locally and organically raised food offers that solution for the United States, if not the entire world. While buying locally, one becomes inextricably linked with the farmers in one's community. It's possible to be on a first name basis with the local butcher, egg farmer, or produce grower, as my family is. Communities grow together in the human miracle that is cuisine, along with economically supporting local farmers. Beyond those perfectly worthy reasons for eating locally grown agriculture, local food also enhances and maintains the local environment. By purchasing food grown within a close proximity to your home, you are reducing the amount of fossil fuels needed in the transportation of said food to your convenience. When buying locally, convenience is right down the street! Another benefit of purchasing local food is the food itself. The level of freshness had when buying local fruit, vegetables, milk, and any other various area specialties is unrivaled at any supermarket. Having confidence that the bunch of carrots in your hand were underground in loamy soil hours before buying them is a basic feeling lost in much of today's world. That feeling, however, is easily eclipsed by the flavor sensation that is that carrot. Fresh and local vegetables, fruits, and meats taste infinitely better than their conventional counterparts who have spent hours in cold storage, sitting on massive transporter trucks, and waiting on the shelves at the grocery store for the disenchanted American shopper to dismally pick them up on a weekly shopping trip.

I have been eating organic and local food for roughly the last ten years. My family and I made the switch to organic and local food for the health benefits as my mother suffers from Crohn's Disease, an intestinal disorder. Essentially, Crohn's Disease causes extreme inflammation in the intestines, to the point where normal nutrient absorption is severely inhibited. Because of this, we decided to make the switch to organic food, as it was healthier and offered a better chance for wellbeing for us. Additionally, we began cultivating our own gardens. I've spent uncountable hours of my summers radically renovating our backyard so as to allow multiple raised-bed gardens and a fruit orchard. During the summer and early fall, we produce enough fruits and vegetables to be able to dramatically reduce our dependence on store-bought fresh food. My passion for food was also implemented this summer while at the International Baccalaureate World Student Conference. While there, I created an IB service project known as "Food for Thought" with my Global Action Team. With Food for Thought, my colleagues and I aim to teach and implement better eating habits in our community through youth education seminars. We came together under a mutual dissatisfaction with American food culture and drafted the skeleton of an organization that hopes to erode the pervasive "food apathy" so commonly found in our everyday lives.

Food is more than just a fulfiller of appetites. Food is culture. Food is passion. Food is emotion. It pained me the time I heard my neighbor's daughter say, "I didn't know you could just pick peas off a plant!" Disconnect with food is one of the largest travesties this generation and world has seen, and yet, it is easily preventable through the proliferation of organic and local food consumption. If more focus was placed on the importance of American connection with the food we eat, food could regain its status as a premier expression of culture and representation of passion.

The Short Essay (for Stanford University)

1.   Stanford students are widely known to possess a sense of intellectual vitality. Tell us about an idea or an experience you have had that you find intellectually engaging.

This summer I was given the opportunity to be a "delegate" at the International Baccalaureate World Student Conference in Corvallis, Oregon. While there, the 300 other students and I formed "Global Action Teams," invented international service projects, and heard from multiple presenters. Perhaps the most impactful speaker was Michael Furdyk. Michael sold his startup computer website MyDesktop.com for millions and used those funds to start TakingITGlobal, a social networking site committed to "Inspire. Inform. Involve," and helping young people reach their activism goals. Simply being in the presence of a young person who has already accomplished more than many people twice his age was one of the most inspiring experiences of my entire life. Speaking with him made me inspired to do more with the world that I live in. It made me look introspectively and ask questions of myself – and not just those related to saving the world, or reconstructing the educational system as Michael is attempting to do. I began asking myself how I can better myself in a holistic sense: how can I maximize my ability to help those around me? How can I maximize my ability to help myself become better? What can I do to differentiate myself? These will be the questions that drive me to strive for higher goals for myself and for the world around me.

2. Virtually all of Stanford's undergraduates live on campus. Write a note to your future roommate that reveals something about you or that will help your roommate – and us – know you better.

Dear Future Roommate-

Hello! ¡Hola! Bonjour! I am genuinely excited to meet you and have plenty of questions to ask, but I'll first spend some time letting you get to know me. I'm almost always reading, researching some random topic, or on an open ended search for new information on the internet. I constantly seek out new knowledge and am easily one of the most curious people I know. It's not just curiosity related to one specific subject either – it's everything and anything that I can get my hands on. If you won't mind the piles of books, looping of Jeopardy! episodes, or the daily "Hey, listen to this...", then I can see us having no issues as roommates.

I am also a very musical person, being a tap dancer and drummer, so naturally, my hands and feet are almost constantly moving. While studying, I listen to music. While cooking, I listen to music. While showering, I listen to music (or revert to making my own, if a stereo is unavailable). If my tapping of fingers, toes, pencils, erasers, eating utensils, drumsticks, tap shoes, or anything else begins to drive you out of your mind, I sincerely apologize. It's not intentional, just a part of who I am.

The bottom line is that I hope we can grow to become more than just roommates. We may be, at first, just sharing a room, but I sincerely hope that we will experience and enjoy Stanford together.

Salud,

CK

3. Tell us what makes Stanford a good place for you.

When thinking of reasons as to why Stanford would be a good place for me as an undergraduate, two reasons immediately come to mind. First, I consider myself an emerging marching band connoisseur. As Drum Major for my high school marching band, I believe that I can discern good from bad, original from commonplace, inspiring and entertaining from nap-inducing. The Leland Stanford Junior *pause* University Marching Band is the quintessence of marching band spirit. How many other college marching bands have award-winning records of their music? How many other college marching bands were revived by an under-the-table deal between band membership and current director in 1963? How many other college marching bands wear red blazers and fishing hats, poke fun at the treatment of the spotted owl's plight, and make giant cardboard robots? Alas, very, very few. Second, Stanford also has the potential to finally quench my undying thirst for foreign language education. Where else can I take Biblical Hebrew, Catalan, Igbo, Armenian, and Lakota all in one place? Exactly. Of all the institutions of higher learning that I am applying to, Stanford's foreign language offerings are incomparable and unmatched. If given the chance to attend Stanford, I would fully utilize the foreign language resources afforded to me and bring a drive and passion hardly matched in any other academic setting.

Colleges granted an alumni interview:

Not applicable

127

Colleges granted acceptance letter:
 Stanford University (early action/decision)

Colleges granted wait list:
 Not applicable

College selected to attend:
 Stanford University (early action/decision)

Student NSD Profile:

Statistics:

 Class Rank: 12 weighted; 11 unweighted Class Size: 579
 GPA: 3.987 (at time of application)
 SAT I:Best total: 2280 (710R, 770W, 800M)
 SAT II: Math 2c: 790 Physics: 700 Amer Lit: 650
 IB/AP: IB Math SL 7 IB Computer sci SL 6

Honors and Awards:

1. International Baccalaureate Diploma Candidate
2. National Honor Society
3. Japanese National Honor Society
4. National Society of High School Scholars
5. 2nd and 3rd place in Youth Art Competition

Extracurricular Activities:

1. Caretaker 1500 hr
2. Employer: Sino Language & Lotus Foundation, Volunteer Teacher. 80hr
3. Chinese, Foreign exchange in China. 240hr
4. National Honor Society President & Website manager. 150hr
5. Martial Arts: Karate Instructor. 240hr
6. Class Treasurer & Fundraiser. 140hr
7. Japanese, Japanese Club. 800hr
8. Computer Science – Java, C# - Group Leader. 180 hr
9. Fundraiser for Amani For Africa, Relay for Life, Key Club – Bulletin Editor. 120hr

10. Tennis. 200hr
11. Drawing. 300hr
12. Math Help: Tutor, Private Tutor. 150hr

The Long Essay:

Evaluate a significant experience, achievement, risk you have taken, or ethical dilemma you have faced and its impact on you.

As I step off a humid bus, I notice the setting is different. It is no longer that of urban Beijing, but the poverty stricken backside of this teaming Chinese metropolis. In fear for my life, I attempt to navigate a maze of back alleyways while diverting my eyes from strangers and drawing (I hope) as little attention to myself as possible. Although Chinese by birth, I definitely do not look local. I finally reach my destination: a migrant school located at the center of this rundown world.

I am here to teach English. I peer around my classroom as I prepare for this first day. I see 17 preteens running around and screaming; I see a bunch of kids having fun. I am heartened by my realization that even though they are progeny of impoverished migrant workers, they vigorously exhibit the glowing innocence of youth. I attempt to speak to them in English. They do not understand. They respond inquisitively "Laoshi, ni shuo shenma?" ("Teacher, what did you say?").

For a moment, I am melancholy. I contemplate the privileged 10-year-olds that I had finished tutoring less than a week before. They had immediately understood almost everything I said. Here, however, teaching children of the same age, but socioeconomically worlds apart, I begin class with a review of the western alphabet...

Although my sojourn involved traveling thousands of miles to teach in a decrepit, decaying school, I am proud to have had the experience. A year before, I participated in a foreign exchange program at Shanghai University to improve my fluency in Mandarin Chinese. It was such a positive experience that I wanted to somehow reciprocate. Consequently, I decided to return to China and teach English.

I was surprised by the level of poverty manifested in some of the communities where I taught. I was often saddened and sometimes scared by my surroundings. Nevertheless, I was determined to fulfill my desire to teach. By exposing Chinese children to the English language, I was knowingly providing an opportunity that they may never have had.

The joy and laughter emanating from the classroom as my pupils began learning a new language brightened a seemingly bleak existence. My students would squeal in delight when I augmented their curriculum by teaching something as basic as a new card game. These children would pluck happiness from the simplest of things. I was thrilled to participate in such innocence.

Yet, I witnessed firsthand the unfortunate and ostensibly insurmountable disparity between distinctly rich and truly poor. Children of means were exposed to and could benefit from a world vastly different from that of their less fortunate counterparts.

Paradoxically, I feel that my students impacted my life much more than I affected theirs. For me, this experience became a watershed; it changed my perception of reality. I look at my life with new perspective. I sincerely understand that I have much, much more than most. I acknowledge that I take for granted more than I should due to the lucky draw of my birth. I decry the fact that difficulties I may experience will never be as overwhelming as those of some (no, most) children I taught.

I no longer dwell on perceived problems. I now take charge of the opportunities afforded me, seeking to derive from them all that I can. I simultaneously strive to enjoy the simple pleasure of living every moment to its fullest!

One day, perhaps, I will be able to repay my indebtedness to my students for catalyzing such change in me.

The Short Essay (for Cornell University, College of Engineering)

Engineers turn ideas (technical, scientific, mathematical) into reality. Tell us about an engineering idea you have or your interest in engineering. Explain how Cornell Engineering can help you further explore this idea or interest. (500 words)

As I look to the future, I see myself as a computer engineer working to develop cutting edge technological innovation in computer architecture, an aspiration of mine that will one day become reality.

My interest in engineering began during my childhood. I was always enthralled with video games, yet differently than most of my friends. I found myself not only playing the games, but also wondering how such games were created. This prompted me to further investigate my curiosity and enroll in a summer course at a local college. It was there I was enlightened by the computer language C++.

However, it was not until high school that I solidified my interest in engineering when I took IB Computer Science. In this class, I learned two more languages (Java and C#), created a major program, and was introduced to working as part of a programming team through group projects. One such project involved redeveloping an archaic computer game called "Hunt the Wumpus." About the same time, I sought to integrate computer science and electrical engineering into one discipline and discovered the existence of computer engineering. It was then that I knew what I wanted to study.

My interest in computer engineering aligns with the academic curriculum and resources offered at Cornell's College of Engineering (Cornell Engineering). As a world-class research university, Cornell

Engineering offers an outstanding education, an atmosphere of intellectual prowess, and most importantly, educators whose primary focus is ensuring success. They instruct classes that range from the rudimentary "Introduction to Circuits for Electrical and Computer Engineers" to the sophisticated "System Architecture, Behavior, and Optimization." My fascination for computer engineering will integrate fully into this environment, leading me one step closer into achieving my goal.

Because I see enormous value in practical experience, I'll participate in Cornell Engineering's co-op program. I'll be exposed to applications of my major while gaining insight pertinent to my chosen career. This distinctive approach to education will allow me to pursue computer engineering at both an academic and an applied level.

During my time at Cornell, I will undoubtedly engender innovative ideas and will be able to explore these ideas utilizing Cornell Engineering's abundant resources. Afforded the opportunity to work together with faculty members such as David Albonesi and Christopher Batten in addition to my fellow peers, my ideas will become real and my interests sated.

Furthermore, Cornell Engineering requires all ECE matriculants to enroll in a Culmination Design Experience Course. Choosing from these unique courses (and one is offered in computer architecture), I'll be able to develop my ability to meet real-life demands through assignments in open-ended engineering design.

Cornell Engineering will definitely be the catalyst that propels my interests and ideas far beyond their current scope. Cultivating my academic passions at Cornell Engineering will propagate my success as a focused scholar, allow me to become a computer engineer and provide the foundation for future leadership in my field.

Colleges granted an alumni interview:

1. Harvard University
2. Massachusetts Institute of Technology
3. Northwestern University
4. Dartmouth College
5. University of Pennsylvania

Colleges granted acceptance letter:

1. Carnegie Mellon
2. Cornell University
3. Duke University
4. Northwestern University
5. University of California, Berkeley
6. University of Washington

<u>Colleges granted wait list</u>:
Not applicable

<u>College selected to attend</u>:
1.   Cornell University

<u>Student CNE Profile</u>:

<u>Statistics</u>:

Class Rank: 10 weighted; 22 unweighted   Class Size: 579
GPA: 3.976 (at time of application)
SAT I:Best total: 2380   (800R, 780W, 800M)
SAT II: Math 2c: 800   Bio: 700   Amer Lit: 780
IB/AP: IB Math SL 7   IB Philosophy SL 6

<u>Honors and Awards</u>:

1.   National Merit Scholar (2010-2011)
2.   National Honor Society Member (2009-2011)
3.   Excellence in journalistic review writing (2010)
4.   Excellence in the French language (2008)
5.   Excellence in mathematics (2008)

<u>Extracurricular Activities</u>:

1.   Co-editor-in-chief of the Nordic News, award-winning student-run publication, 13 hrs/wk, 35 wks/yr (2010-2011)
2.   Volunteer/intern with Projects Abroad South Africa-Human Rights office, 30 hrs/wk, 3 wks/yr (2010)
3.   Founder and president of International Service Club, 2 hrs/wk, 30 wks/yr (2010-2011)
4.   Student participant at International Baccalaureate World Student Conference, 25 hrs/wk, 1 wk/yr (2010)
5.   Volunteer at Little Bit Therapeutic Riding Center, 2 hrs/wk, 20 wks/yr (2008-2010)
6.   Volunteer/intern at Tulalip Reservation Medical Clinic, 16 hrs/wk, 5 wks/yr (2009)
7.   Student at University of Dijon summer language program, 30 hrs/wk, 3 wks/yr (2010)
8.   President of French Club, 1 hr/wk, 30 wks/yr (2010-2011)

9.   LINK leader, 6 hrs/wk, 3 wks/yr (2009-2011)
10. Relay for Life team captain, 2 hrs/wk, 8 wks/yr (2008-2009)

The Long Essay:

Evaluate a significant experience, achievement, risk you have taken, or ethical dilemma you have faced and its impact on you.

"Attempted murder. Two counts." Paul was only sixteen. I tried not to react as he told me why he was in Bonnytoun Juvenile Detention Center.

"Are you aware that you have the right to legal representation in court?"

My questions and his answers continued. I completed the form that would go into our data collection; the Projects Abroad South Africa Human Rights office would later tabulate how many of the juvenile detainees were aware of their constitutional rights and if those rights were being violated.

"Excuse me," Paul interrupted. "Where are you from?"

"The United States," I told him. He looked at me for a moment.

"Do you live in a nice house there, with a nice life? Did you pay lots of money to come here? Why do you think you can come here and ask me these questions?"

I was struck silent by the justified venom in his voice.

Before my first visit to the townships, the poorest areas of South Africa and remnants of the apartheid era, one of the office heads told me to watch my back but keep my head down. Eye contact, he said, could be the end of you.

"You know nothing," he had told all the volunteers. "You all feel proud because you got through airport security by yourselves. Soon you will learn what it really means to help people."

As I walked between the rows of metal shacks, however, I was met only by warmth. A man huddled in a cardboard hut with nothing but an extra set of clothing smiled at me and held his hand out—as I guiltily began reaching for the money in my pocket, I realized he only wished to shake my hand. My immediate assumption that he had been asking for charity was a direct result of the uninformed perspectives I brought with me to the township; Paul had asked me his pointed questions because he knew about the stereotypes I had brought with me.

I listened to a woman who had felt her baby die in her arms as she fled the Congo. She said she was still grateful for receiving a chance at a new life, and I was overwhelmed by a rush of shame. I had not even known what a township was prior to my arrival, yet I had felt that I had the right to come to South Africa and tell these people I was there to change their lives. I had felt that people should consider me noble and altruistic after hearing a suitable number of moving and emotional stories from my trip. I had wanted Paul to smile and thank me for coming. I had been looking for glorification, for self-gratification, and I realized that the office head was right: I knew nothing, and I did not deserve to look these people in the eye. Perhaps that was why I had been told to keep my gaze cast down.

Before my trip, hardship, dirt roads and shacks full of debris had held a peculiar glamor to me; they had represented a world I did not know or understand. My time in South Africa showed me that I had signed up to be a 'volunteer' in a fit of narcissism and ignorance. While I was in Cape Town, I learned that my work was an honor, not a right. Anyone who strives to help others must have the capacity to grow, and I found that the South Africans I met, in this regard, did not need my help. In spite of their continuing suffering, they possessed a hope I have seen nowhere else.

The optimism and humility I encountered made me abjectly ashamed of many of the values I had brought with me. The young men in Bonnytoun told me that all they had ever wanted was to go to school; I whine about the workload that comes with my education. The children I met in the townships could have been shot in the streets if they did not move quickly enough; I complain about the ennui of my suburban neighborhood.

The people I met in South Africa taught me that I must make myself worthy of the resources I hope to receive, and that I must earn the privilege of using those resources to aid the people who are being wronged all over the world. If education were granted by merit rather than means, every child I saw in Cape Town would be in school. I now wish to justify the schooling I have received by making the most of my future education, the education those children may never have.

As for Paul, I regret that I had not realized what I know now when he confronted me. I could not answer him at the time; I shuffled my papers and changed the subject. If I could go back, I would tell Paul that he was right, that I had come to South Africa for all the wrong reasons. I would thank him for reminding me of how grateful I should be, and for ensuring that I will now work to be worthy of his respect and not just my own.

The Short Essay (for Harvard University)

Zazen is a matter of training yourself to become a Buddha; rather, to return to being a Buddha, for you are one from the beginning.
-In Search of the Missing Ox, Buddhist parable

It is strange to think that most of us no longer know how to enter our most natural state: that of being, being without thought or self-consciousness. Years and years of conditioning have buried our innate state of pure mind. We have been taught to think and feel at every moment: modern-day society demands that we are in constant interaction with our surroundings.

The way back is difficult. Recently, I have been trying to find it through zazen meditation, a Buddhist tradition that focuses on breathing practices. Mindful breath: I must be aware of every breath that goes through me. It sounds simple at first, but it is surprising how little control we now have over our minds.

About three years ago, I began having frequent panic attacks: I felt the walls of my world closing in on me. I saw how very tiny I was in the universe, how I was nothing but a speck of dust that would disappear quickly, how unimportant I was in the grand scheme of things. I saw no resolution to this apparent problem until I began meditating.

Meditation has shown me that my insignificance is not something to fear or attempt to reject: principles of Buddhism have shown me that the only grand scheme that exists is my own mind. When I meditate, I catch a glimpse of how expansive the world can be. The balance and harmony I attempt to practice in zazen meditation is present everywhere I look. I may be a small variable in the universe, but the clarity of mind that comes with meditation has shown me that my actions can change things—my being in itself is irrelevant. We have been trained and conditioned to process and analyze at all times—we have simultaneously been made to believe that we, as people, must be important.

In the rediscovery of balance in the world is the acknowledgement that everything is equally important. Any attempt I would make at rejecting my equality with the rest of the world would result in unbalance and confusion. I used to see the world as a place over which I must exert control, but I now know it as an environment which I, in my original state of pure mind, help to balance.

The panic attacks stopped as I returned to my natural state through meditation. I think that many forms of today's social injustice are magnified versions of those panic attacks: I now see that my actions should help to remedy those imbalances. We all have the potential to do so: we just have to return to our original zen.

Colleges granted an alumni interview:

1. Brown University
2. Harvard University
3. Princeton University
4. Tufts University
5. Yale University

Colleges granted acceptance letter:

1. Harvard University
2. Tufts University
3. University of Washington

Colleges granted wait list:

1. Brown University
2. Columbia University

College selected to attend:

1. Harvard University

Chapter 12. The Alumni Interview and the Wait List

Once the applications are gone, life goes back to normal. What a relief! But, three weeks after sending off the applications, anxiety settles in. Will the student be accepted? Will the student be rejected? Will the student be deferred? Does the college or university need more information? To find out, a student should periodically check his or her private account on the website of each college where the student applied. Also, many colleges notify applicants about application status by email, so checking email frequently is important. Well, at least these checks are important for people who are nervous about their application status.

Shaudi was totally relaxed after the application process. He did not check his accounts on college websites and he had more than 600 unread emails. We had even asked him to check with colleges to ensure his application was complete. His typical replies were: "I'm too busy with my homework" or "I have a paper due tomorrow morning." Finally, we sat down with him to check his accounts. Shaudi had received alumni interview emails directly from alumni from all East Coast colleges except two to which he had applied. Also, two colleges had not received his SAT scores from the College Board despite our requests and payments. The deadline had long passed. An incomplete application would not be considered. We could not dwell on that, though. We helped Shaudi line up alumni interviews and encouraged him to concentrate on those.

Tip: After the application is in, a parent should ensure a student checks all accounts a college or university could use to update the application's status.

An alumni interview is a good indicator as well as a bad indicator. A strong applicant with a high probability of acceptance will not need the interview, and a weak applicant with a low probability of acceptance would be rejected without the need for it. It is the borderline applicant who gets the interview. A good report from an alumni will not influence the decision of the admissions committee, but a negative report will certainly spoil a student's chance for admission. Most alumni interviewers do not know the student's information from the application forms, although some do see the application forms before the meeting. When Lauda was applying, he received alumni interview invitations from two highly selective East Coast colleges (one accepted him and the other rejected him), whereas Shaudi received invitations from five highly selective East Coast colleges.

Tip: Alumni interviews are for borderline applicants.
Students should take them seriously.

Alumni who conduct interviews are typically people who happen to live or work in the student's area. Some hold the meeting in their office, while others perform the interview in a local coffee shop, a restaurant, or a public library. The meetings are mostly informal. There are no right or wrong answers, but there are some answers that make common sense to an adult, yet evade the mind of a teenager. For example, one of Lauda's interviewers asked him how he would decide which college to attend. Lauda replied, "It's a family decision." A better answer would have been: "The academic rigor at your college inspires me," or "Professor Smith's research topic on nanotechnology really appeals to me." But, Lauda did get an acceptance letter from that college. This speaks to how inconsequential alumni interviews can be.

Still, when Shaudi's time came for alumni interviews, we thought it would be a good idea to prepare him more than we had Lauda. We searched online for alumni interview questions and topics, and compiled a list for a practice session at home. These dry runs did illicit some interesting answers, some innocent and some immature. For example, we asked Shaudi, "Why do you want to go to college?" His answer was, "Because I can find a better job and make more money." This is absolutely true and probably every family's reasoning and purpose for pushing a student to study hard. But, there are many other good and true answers justifying the importance of a college education. "College education will prepare me for a better chance of success in my future career" is a true and good answer yet appears more mature. We did remind Shaudi there are no right or wrong answers, but he should think about a question before answering it, and then elaborate on the topic. We also wanted him to be able to make a good impression before the interview even started and after it ended. Therefore, we told him all interviews have a before, during, and after.

Before the interview:

1. Arrive earlier than the interviewer to familiarize the setting and calm down the nervousness.
2. Survey the room and, when he or she arrives, the interviewer.
3. Have a firm handshake; it shows confidence.
4. Speak with enthusiasm about your passions.
5. Subtly, steer the conversation by presenting several topics in answering a question. This allows the interviewer to choose the next question easily.
6. Make eye contact, hold your arms and hands open, and have relaxed legs and feet.
7. Sit straight, in the front half of the seat to show eagerness.
8. Lean forward to show your motivation.
9. Help the interviewer complete the evaluation form by answering questions with catchy/memorable phrases you have practiced at home.
10. Never give a single-word or single-sentence answer. Always elaborate and tell why and a lesson learned.

<u>During an interview</u>, expect these questions:

General:

1. Tell me a little bit about yourself. How do you describe yourself to someone who doesn't know you?
2. What makes you unique?
3. Give me three adjectives or objects you would use to describe yourself.
4. What is your greatest passion?
5. What fun activities or hobbies do you do in your spare time? How do you balance time between life and school/work?
6. How do you spend a typical afternoon after school? Evening? Weekend?
7. What do you see as your greatest strength or weakness? What do you do best?
8. What is your long-term goal?
9. What will you do in 10 years, or after graduation, and how will you achieve that?
10. Tell me something about your family.
11. How would your friends describe you?
12. What are you most proud of?

High school:

1. What is your favorite class in high school? What is your most challenging class? Why?
2. If you had high school to do over again, what might you do differently?
3. What mark do you feel you have left on your school?
4. What is the most important thing you learned in high school?
5. What high school experience was the most important to you?

6. What is your goal for your senior year?

7. Is there anything you would like to tell me about your transcript?

Extracurricular activities:

1. What volunteer work or community service work have you done or are you doing?
   a. Why do you do that?
   b. What do you learn from it?

2. Of the volunteer work you have done, what had the most influence on you and why? What have you found most satisfying?

3. Do you participate in any team, or club, or group outside of class room?

4. Do you do any paid job?

5. What book would you recommend to me or someone else? What book, not required by school, have you read recently?

Knowledge of the College:

1. Why are you considering our college? What attracts you to our college?

2. Why should we admit you? Why do you think this college is a good match for you?

3. Have you visited the campus? What impressed you?

4. How did you learn about our college?

5. Where else are you applying and why?

6. What do you hope to major in and why?

7. What will you contribute to our campus life?

8. What do you want to get out of your college experience?

Tricky questions:

1. Did you Google me before coming here?
2. Why do you or why would anyone want a higher education?
3. How do you define "success"?
4. If you could talk with any living or dead person, who would it be and why?
5. What events have been crucial in your life? Who is your hero, or who do you admire the most, or who had the greatest influence on you? Why?

Tests of maturity and integrity (hard for students at this stage in life):

1. Give an example of a time when you had to solve a difficult problem. What was the problem and how did you go about resolving the issue?

2. Give an example of important feedback you have received (positive or negative). What made it important? How did it impact you? What did you do with it?

3. What has been your greatest disappointment to date and what did you do with it?

4. Describe a situation in which you felt misjudged.

5. Describe an experience in which communication proved difficult.

6. Compared to others you know, how well do you handle pressure? Criticism? Failure?

7. Describe a situation in which you felt you could not connect with

someone, and why. What could you have done to allow for better connection?

8. Describe a situation in which you had to step outside your comfort zone. What did you learn from that experience?

9. Which of your character traits do you find most difficult to portray in an interview?

10. When was the last time you made a mistake, and what did you do about it?

11. Talk about a significant challenge you have encountered.

12. What is your learning style?

13. How do you see life changing when you are a college student?

14. How do you want to be remembered by others?

15. How do you resolve conflict with your peers? At home? In the classroom?

In the end of any interview, most interviewers include the polite question, "Do you have any questions to ask me?" or "Is there anything you want to share that we haven't discussed?" A student should have prepared a few questions to use here to engage the interviewer in conversation such as "what advice could you give me to make the most out of my time there?"; or "if you could do it again, what would you do differently?". This is also an opportune time to provide information that is important but was not mentioned during the interview. This is a chance for a student to provide a summary of himself or herself to showcase how the student would fit well in the school.

After the interview:

Once home, it is always polite to write a quick thank-you note to the interviewer. This note, ideally, arrives before the interviewer completes the interview report card. The interview report card typically rates students from 1 to 5 in various categories, explains a *New York Times* article. The article, "College Prep: The Alumni Interview," by Glenn C. Altschuler, published November 10, 2002, numbers and details the categories, too: "(1) preparation for interview, (2) intellectual promise, (3) personal promise, (4) conversational ability and (5) maturity/motivation. There is also a brief summary of strengths and weaknesses, and whether the candidate is strongly recommended or not recommended." For this book, I asked several alumni interviewers what they were looking for from a student in an alumni interview. Typical answers included: "We aren't judging whether the answer is right or wrong, rather we are trying to get a feel about an aspect of the student which is not obvious from the paperwork," and "The enthusiasm at the college, the drive to succeed in college, the affability to classmates on campus."

Even if a student is not accepted to a college after an alumni interview – as eventually happened to Shaudi – we still believe home practice is a good idea. Good interviewing skills provide a lifelong benefit. Whether for a future graduate school application, job application, or interview for a promotion, it is always better to practice being able to connect with people and make a good first good impression. If professional movie actors and actresses need multiple attempts to get a perfect frame of film, then, to achieve a good interview rapport, we ordinary, honest people obviously need a lot more practice.

> *Tip: Practice for the before, during, and after of alumni interviews provides a lifelong benefit.*

Once alumni interviews are finished, the college application process is truly over. What follows is even more anxious waiting. Neither Lauda nor Shaudi had ever picked up the mail, but they willingly took the mail home every day as they awaited their acceptance or rejection letters. Some colleges send this news by email or through the online account, but many stick to the tradition of regular, postal mail. A large, fat envelope indicates good news and a small, thin envelope signals bad news. During the weekend, the boys slept in so we picked up the mail.

Lauda learned his happy news at high school. He checked his account on his dream school's website the minute the result was posted. He immediately called from school to inform June: "I got in!" June then relayed the news to me. It was a relief. Lauda had been quite nervous because many of his classmates had been receiving good news in the previous few days, but he had had none. Hearing good news from other students just made his, and our, anxieties worse. We tried to appear cool, but we were churning with anxiety. After the first good news, Lauda received many other acceptance letters from other colleges. But, with his dream school admission secure, these other letters did not excite Lauda. There were some good offers too, such as a five-year master's degree program and secure research grants for each summer. But nothing changed his mind. He was ready to live his dream.

Shaudi had an even more emotional roller coaster ride as he awaited his letters. His friends began reporting good news from different colleges, but Shaudi had none. One week had passed since his safety school had sent out letters. Many of his classmates had been accepted, but Shaudi continued not to receive any news. We parents became worried too. June was agitated. My heart was like a sandbag hanging in midair: heavy, yet not secure. Then came the first letter. It was for a wait list. We learned this from the parent of one of Shaudi's classmates. Shaudi did not tell us until a few days later, for fear of disappointing us. I was upset, and I told him so: "You need to tell us so we can take some action. You haven't yet received any acceptance letters, so we need to grasp any hope, even the wait list."

"The wait list is useless," Shaudi replied. "No one from last year's wait list at that college got in."

June could not sit still, so she contacted our private college counselor. The counselor discussed the situation with Shaudi, and advised him to write a polite letter to further strengthen his application and to accept the wait list spot. Then, one morning when I was going to work, I noticed a letter in the trash bin in the garage. It was a rejection letter from another college. Shaudi had picked up the mail the previous evening and thrown away the letter without telling us the bad news. When I came home after work, I showed the letter to June and we decided we need to have a discussion with Shaudi.

"Who are the people willing to sacrifice for your well-being?" I asked.

"You guys," Shaudi answered.

"When you have difficulties, who will do everything to help you?" I pressed on.

"You guys," Shaudi murmured.

"Then why didn't you tell us all the news? We learned about your first wait list from someone else's parent and we learned about the rejection from the trash bin. Where is your logic? " I demanded. Shaudi fell to silence.

For the next days to weeks, Shaudi showed us a few more wait list letters, and he followed the private college counselor's advice and replied with a nice letter to each one. I called a colleague whose daughter, Jenny, had been wait-listed two years before and asked my colleague for advice. Jenny had provided more information and recommendation letters, one from a faculty member at the college and another from a well-known scientist. Jenny and her parents even made a special trip to meet with the admissions officer. But, no luck. It turns out most colleges do not encourage a trip specifically to meet with an admissions officer, nor do the colleges want more letters. "We can not wait at home to be emotionally paralyzed by these strings of bad news and anxieties." I said to June. We contemplated making a special trip to visit the few colleges that had sent Shaudi a letter notifying him he was on the wait list. But, a plane ticket to the East Coast was around $1,000 per person for a last-minute booking. I had planned to take a week off during spring break for East Coast campus visits. But, without a sure acceptance, we needed to think about the trip. June was still monitoring ticket prices when Shaudi, finally, received good news. Then, in the next three days, more good news followed. Soon, Shaudi had four acceptance letters. We breathed a sigh of relief.

"Since Shaudi is on spring break, why don't we let him go to visit the campuses by himself?" June suggested. "Forget the wait-list colleges. He can go where he is accepted."

Shaudi and I agreed to this plan. He eagerly contacted the colleges and carefully made arrangements with friends and with host students to stay in campus dormitories. June and I booked a week at a resort in Canada to relieve our stress. Still, this would be the first time Shaudi took a long-distance trip by himself. As parents, we were certainly worried. Since this was a cross-country trip with two layovers each way, and changes in time zone, we worried he might oversleep in an airport and miss a transfer flight. We instructed Shaudi to text message us at every stop on the way. We kept his itinerary on hand. If we did not receive his message when we thought we should, we would text or call him. Shaudi was a good boy and adhered to the instructions very well. The first text message was "boarding" from our local airport, and the second was "landed" at 3 a.m., our time. The next message was at 5 a.m., "boarding" again. Once he arrived at a campus, we were able to relax and enjoy the resort. When he came home, Shaudi was exhausted and slept for two days. A week later he took a similar trip to visit a college on the West Coast. He finalized his enrollment decision soon after. None of the wait list colleges offered a follow-up acceptance letter.

This is sadly typical. The chance of acceptance from a wait list is quite dismal. The chances are further dimmed in view of the non-published statistics on acceptance quotas. Typically, 25-30% of acceptances go to legacies (students with a parent or grandparent attended the same college); 10-15% go to underrepresented minorities (such as African American and Hispanic American but not Asian); 10% go to development to cultivate future donors, and 15% go to athletes[7]. Furthermore, when the first round of acceptance letters are sent out, colleges invite more students than the college has available spots, based on calculations from past enrollment rates as discussed in Chapter 10. In recent years, more admissions offices are yielding to the pressure of popular, public opinion on college rankings stirred up by magazines. This is because enrollment rates are one of the parameters publication use in their rank calculations. A higher enrollment rate raises a college or university's rank. Consequently, universities send fewer acceptance letters in their first round, expecting a higher percentage of students to enroll. But, to secure enough incoming students, colleges and universities place a large number of students on the wait list. So, using the earlier example in Chapter 10, the less popular college could send 2,500 letters for the 1,500 spots to get an enrollment rate of 60%, a good jump into the league of popular colleges. But in practice, there is a chance the college may not get enough students to fill the incoming freshman class. So, the college grows its pool of wait-listed students. For the wait-listed student, however, the chance of moving from wait list to acceptance shrinks

148

because wait lists are larger than they were in the past. After the May 1st deadline for putting down an enrollment deposit, admissions officers would know how many students they need from the wait list to fill empty spots. They then start calling students who had accepted the wait-list condition. Many colleges do not organize a wait list by first come, first serve. Instead, the college sends an admission letter if the student promises to come if offered a spot. This increases the enrollment rate from the wait list. We are sure not many colleges play this game, but it does seem to be becoming harder and harder to move from a wait list to a seat in the freshman class.

Tip: Do not count on admission from a wait list.

But perseverance and extra efforts can pay off. A true story from Kira, daughter of my colleague Ginny, about her success in getting into dream college from the waiting list may shed some light and hope for many students in similar situation.

Kira applied to seven different colleges, most of them small, liberal arts schools. Soon, thick admission packets started to arrive. Then, one day, a small, thin, envelope arrived from her first-choice college. She opened it and was devastated. She was wait listed.

"Why wasn't I good enough?" Kira cried. "I had all the extracurricular activities, my SAT/ACT scores were competitive, I had a strong admission essay, and I am going to be co-valedictorian of my high school class! Sarah and Emi, two of my fellow valedictorians received acceptance letters from the same college. Why did they get in and I didn't?"

Kira immediately filled out and returned the postcard indicating she wanted to be placed on the wait list, but her parents reminded her she needed to do more. Kira understood the points and determined she would do something to make the admissions department notice her.

First, Kira wrote a two-page letter explaining why the college was her number one choice and what made her different from all other applicants. In the letter, she talked about unique components of the college's academic and campus life programs she was looking forward to participating in. She also wanted to emphasize what made her different from all the other white, middle class, academically successful girls who applied. She explained that she was very attracted to the way the college was part of its surrounding community and was involved in community service. She then gave details of some of the recent service experiences and accomplishments listed on her original application. She concluded:

> *In closing I believe my story has shown evidence of motivation, discipline, imagination, creativity, leadership, and maturity. I have a unique enthusiasm and excitement to bring to all I will do at your college, from classes, to community service, to campus life. I have high expectations of myself and demand excellence from myself. I don't do anything half way. These kinds of characteristics will make a difference at your school.*
>
> *In the past year I have visited your school twice and every time I feel intuitively it is the place for me. I would like to be number one on your waiting list. I am very excited about the prospect of being a student at your school. Thank you for taking time to reconsider my application.*

The letter was powerful. I can not imagine any admissions officer would ignore her plea. But, Kira wasn't finished. Kira also enlisted help from her friend Emi, who had been accepted to the college, to write a letter on Kira's behalf explaining why she thought Kira should be accepted. The admissions department now had two letters explaining why Kira would make an excellent addition to their college community. However, letters can get filed away and forgotten.

Next, Kira had to make sure the admissions office did not forget about her. Kira called the admissions office repeatedly. First, she called first to check ensure they received her letter. Then, she called several times to check on the status of her application. In mid-May, Kira went as a student volunteer on a medical mission to Latin America. She even called the college from Peru. Kira was trying to show the college that it was her one and only choice.

Kira had by then done everything she could to get herself to the top of the waitlist. The only thing left to do was be patient, but then she got a lucky break.

Kira's high school guidance counselor called her and four other students to the counselor's office. The president of Kira's first-choice college would be visiting the high school and the counselor wanted Kira and the other students to give the president a tour. The other four students had already been accepted and were planning on attending the college in the fall. Kira was still waiting and hoping. When Kira introduced herself to the president, she told him this. The president said he wanted to talk to Kira after the tour. Kira ended up having a one-on-one interview with him. Kira repeated what she wrote in her compelling letter, which, of course, the president had not seen. At the end of the impromptu interview, the president said he did not have any say in admissions decisions, but that he would put in a good word for Kira.

When Kira got home from school that afternoon, there was a message on the answering machine. She had been accepted! When Kira's mom asked the admissions department about the acceptance, the admissions officer said the college president had nothing to do with it. Was it a coincidence that Kira was accepted on the same day she met with him? Regardless, in the end, it was persistence and a bit of luck that helped Kira get into her dream school and have a fantastic four years there.

As George Washington noted in his diary after winning many battles against the superior British forces in unlikely odds by any imaginations, "Perseverance have done wonders in all ages." It still does wonders today and does so in college admission process.

Tip: Perseverance has done wonders in all ages, and does so in college admission process

---

Chapter 13. Sending Students off to College

13.1. The last stretch of high school life: theirs and ours

After hearing from his desired college, Lauda's life was immediately more pleasant. He still needed to complete his course work and keep up his GPA. He continued to work hard, as usual. Before we knew it, we were sitting at his high school graduation. When Lauda had applied to college, he had the highest class rank. But, he walked in second place at his graduation, another student having eclipsed his GPA. Lauda was the salutatorian. One by one, students came to the stage to shake hands with the principal and receive the cover of their diplomas. There were numerous speeches. The principal smiled as she told her students, "After we break out of here tonight, you are part of the history of our high school, and we are no longer responsible for your academic conduct."

I realized, with a shock, it was true.

"Lauda has become part of the history of the high school," I whispered to June, "He won't be going to school tomorrow morning."

I was proud, but sad, as I thought about my son completing high school. But, once the graduation ceremony ended, the other students did not appear to share my wistfulness. Groups of young men and women showed off their caps and gowns as their parents' cameras flashed. The new graduates were all excited. They did not seem to appreciate that that night was the last chance for them to be together as a class.

After the photo-ops, the students climbed onto a bus bound for a "secret place" for a whole-night party. An organizing committee of volunteer parents had selected the location for the party, had collected fees, had rented space, and were tight-lipped throughout the process. I was curious, having never experienced anything like this celebration, so I volunteered as one of the 18 chaperone parents to join the party. There were two chaperones per bus to watch over the newly graduated teenagers. There was no pushing or fighting for better seats, but there was enormous amount of talking and loud noise on the bus.

"On a regular school day, the bus driver intervenes to stop all the noise and yelling," explained the other chaperone parent, who had been born in the United States. "But, today, the driver has to endure the noise just like we do."

The bus wandered along the suburban streets, then to the highway, and then along the narrow streets in downtown Seattle. I got lost tracking the route, just as I always did downtown, even in daytime. I became more and more curious about the party's "secret place." The bus driver must have purposely detoured, as it seemed like it had been a long time since the bus had left the ceremony site. The windows in the bus could not be opened, and the smell from the teenagers' sweat and oil glands, fueled by their peak hormone levels, was getting stronger and stronger and more and more difficult for the adults to bear as the summer night dragged on. I wished for the destination to be near. The students seemed not to care about the smell or the noise or where they were going. They just kept shouting and laughing and talking. Finally, a cheer erupted in the bus when we finally stopped along a curb.

"It's the Game Factory!"

The students all leapt up to get off the bus. We chaperone parents stepped out of the bus first to take some deep breaths of fresh air. Then, to make sure each student was counted, one chaperone stood at the door to the Game Factory and the other stood at the door of the bus. The students exited the bus speedily. After all the students from all eight buses entered the building, the Game Factory doors were locked. The lead parent of the organizing committee held the key. Thus, the fun night started. There were bathrooms, and a large supply of food and drinks. Students swarmed an array of electronic games, rides, climbing walls, car races, and other machines. Chaperone parents stood at various stations and rotated every few hours. By 3 a.m., about a third of the students were sleeping on the floors or leaning against the walls without any order of column or row. It looked like a grim battlefield of a 22nd century war fought via video game under fluorescent lighting. There were several couples obviously in romantic relationships who were begging the chaperone parents guarding the fire door entrance, which was not locked, to let them leave the building. The couples were not allowed to leave. One couple became hostile to a parent, and the lead chaperone had to intervene and threaten to call the couple's parents to calm them down. By 6 a.m., not a single student was alert enough to help clean the floor. The chaperone parents had to clean up everything and prod the lethargic students back onto the buses. This took substantially longer than unloading the students had back in the early evening. When we returned to the high school, I drove Lauda home. We both slept until the afternoon.

Five years later, when Shaudi's graduation night party came, I did not volunteer as a chaperone parent. Shaudi's party was at a family fun place near an amusement park between the airport and downtown. He came home in the morning, making both our sons "history" of the same high school.

Both times, the "secret location party" mix of exhaustion and fun appropriately capped the senior year. For both our sons, the final year of high school had brought the stress of college applications, but also the joy of the homecoming dance, the prom, and, finally, the graduation party. I would sometimes grumble about these things. Shaudi, especially, was extremely generous. For prom, in addition to dinner and a gift for his date, he spent $100 to rent a personally tailored tuxedo; $30 for a fresh-cut, purple boutonniere; and $60 per person for a one-hour group ride in a limo. I mumbled after seeing each purchase.

"It is silly to spend so much money on this kind of thing," I told June. "The Men's Warehouse stores make such a high profit from high school seniors. It is a billion-dollar business."

June would come to Shaudi's defense.

"This is a fun, life experience," she would argue. "High school is a very special time in one's life. Let him have his way. Besides, I already told Shaudi that not all students could afford these expenses, and he should feel blessed."

Then I would indulge myself by reflecting on my own "life experience" in high school.

I attended Baofeng First High School (where Lauda did his volunteer work as described in his long essay in Chapter 7). Baofeng was also where the county government was located. My high school was the only high school for the whole county, which had a population of 200,000. The high school was founded in the 1950's, but was closed in the 1960's during the Cultural Revolution. In 1978, when Deng Xiao Ping returned to Chinese communist party leadership, science and education became more of a national priority over Marxism. I was lucky to be in the first class of students selected county-wide, by merit, to attend the school 20 miles from my home. I would stay at school for four weeks at a time, living in a dormitory, only going home when my food supplies ran out. To get to school from home, I walked three miles to a bus station, then took a 15-mile bus ride when I could catch or afford the bus. More often, to save a bus ticket, like many kids, I would jump up, grab onto, and climb into the open bed of a truck transporting coal, moving at full speed. This maneuver was like a movie stunt, but it was a necessity. Once the truck reached Baofeng, I would hang off the rear bumper and jump down into the street, while the truck still was moving at full speed. The drivers never knew of the passengers they had "helped." There were a few occasions when students were thrown off a truck when the truck's rear wheels hit a large bump. Students suffered concussions and fractures. For me, once I safely climbed off a bus or jumped off a truck, the last portion of the trip to school was another two-mile walk. Sometimes, I borrowed a bicycle from a city classmate who came from a more affluent family. I would have to pay the boy back by helping him with his homework or taking his turn to wipe the classroom floor.

Most of the students were like me, from the poor countryside. The only way to change our social status was through study and a college education. Morning bell was a 6 a.m. Lights off in the dormitory was at 10 p.m. Our first activity after morning bell was to run the high school's unpaved 400-meter track. Students rotated the duty to spray water on the track to dampen the earth so dust wouldn't cover every pupil. Every one of the high school's 900 students would be lined up along the track. Every 50 students (20% girls and 80% boys) made up one squad, led by a class president. The class president would check names and record absentees every morning. I was a class president for most of my high school career, and I led most of the morning runs and name checks. Despite diligent spraying, the dust still flew as 900 pairs of shoes completed five laps. Then, there was a morning self-study period, followed by breakfast. Formal classes started at 8 a.m. and lasted until noon. Afternoon classes were from 2 p.m. to 5 p.m. After supper, there was another self-study period. There was not enough time to complete homework. Students used a precious, ten-minute break between classes to catch up on assignments.

Bathroom time was for reading. Meal time was for discussing equations with close friends.

Weekends were as intensive as weekdays, except once every month when I had to go home to bring back bags of wheat or corn to exchange for meal tickets. I would also bring bottles of pickled mustard root slices or sautéed chili powders to flavor the corn flour buns and cornmeal soup I received for three meals per day. One pound of grain would get a 0.8 pound of meal ticket. One steamed bun took 0.2 pounds off the ticket and a bowl of cornmeal soup took 0.1 pound off the ticket. That was one meal. A 30-pound bag of grain would serve me for about a month. Students with similarly poor home conditions tended to group together and did not mind sharing what they had. Occasionally, when relatives came to Baofeng for other business, they would pass along an extra one or two bags of grain, saving me a trip home, so I could spend the time on schoolwork. Sometimes, I could use my father's leftover universal food ration ticket to exchange for a school meal ticket, also a way to avoid another trip. My treats were wheat-flour buns and rice soup once a week.

The dormitory was one, large rectangular room with one entrance and two windows on the front wall for all 40 boys in the student corps. There were two, raised clay platforms with a path in between. A single platform against the back wall had 25 sleeping lots. The platform against the front wall, divided into two sections by the entrance, hosted the remainder of the 15 students. Students lay next to each other as we shared body heat. There was no coal stove to warm the dormitory as there was in the classroom. The temperature ranged from -5° C to +5° C. I had frostbite on my feet every winter. Occasionally, we had rice or wheat straw to put on our sleeping boards. Our squad's homeroom teacher checked the dormitory behavior every night after lights off and listened outside the window to identify if a "sleep spoiler" would receive disciplinary remarks the next day. Because we had no fruits or vegetables in our diets, we had chronic constipation and food would ferment by our bowel bacteria for a longer time. If one student farted, the air of the whole dorm became poisonous. This meant everyone had to get up to fan the air away. Our bodies fed the same lice in the winter and the same fleas in the summer. Still, every one of us was fairly healthy. We were countryside boys toughened by hard living conditions. No one had an excuse to be absent due to insect-transmitted diseases. My longest absence was one week following increasing weakness, fatigue and shortness of breath. The school nurse saw how pale I was and sent me to a clinic in the town center. There, I saw a traditional, Chinese medicine practitioner. I was diagnosed as "Yin Xu." The Western medical term would be malnutrition. I received two bottles of pills and I went home to be nursed by my mother with wheat flour buns and soups. I took the pills three times a day, as instructed. After one week, I went back to school.

Now, as an American Board of Internal Medicine-certified physician with a specialty in hematology and oncology, I know I had anemia due to folic acid deficiency. The medications were probably folic acid and vitamin B12.

So, the "life experience" Lauda and Shaudi encountered in their high school years left me with frustration with their expenses and little sympathies for their hardships. One weekend afternoon, before Lauda departed for Stanford University, June was organizing his high school papers and cleaning up his things, intending to donate his childhood toys such as Legos and Super Mario games, when Lauda commented he wanted to keep those toys to show his children what "hardship" he had been through. In relative terms, he did have fewer entertainment devices than his classmates. June and I laughed at his perceived hardship. We admitted that time had changed and the definition for hardship changes with different eras and locations. We agreed our sons should have some fun time and activities. This helped me accept the change and more willingly dip into my wallet when our sons wanted financial support for their parties and living expenses before and during college.

> *Tip: Even if their experience differs from yours, if your budget can afford it, help your children enjoy the fun of high school and, later, of college.*

13.2. A new life in the family

When Lauda was getting ready to leave for college and Shaudi asked for a dog, I jumped into the idea even without consulting June. Shaudi and Lauda had been very close during their growing up. It was Lauda who asked for a brother to play with him. They slept in the same queen-size bed, and later the same bunk beds until Lauda reached high school and their sleeping pattern differed. We had always traveled together. When in a hotel, they liked to stay together in the room to watch cable TV, as we did not have cable at home. Shaudi accepted Lauda's advice and suggestions more readily than ours. They never fought or argued with each other.

> *Tip: If the household includes a younger child or children, keep in mind their needs as the older sibling prepares to leave for college.*

"It will be hard for Shaudi to adapt to being the only child at home when Lauda goes off to college," I said to June, trying to explain my thinking for eagerly agreeing to Shaudi's request for a dog.

"I agree with your reasoning and understand that Shaudi will have separation anxiety when Lauda leaves. But did you talk to him about privileges and responsibilities?" June asked. "This would be a new life in the family. I never had a dog and don't know how to raise one."

I countered: "We did not have any knowledge on raising children before, we have two now and they appear to be growing up as fine young men."

I then added my promises to help to feed and walk the dog.

June began to research what type of dog to get. We watched dog shows on TV, we attended dog shows in real life, and we borrowed piles of books on dogs from the public library. I took notes, as always.

"We never read or studied this much before and after Lauda was born," I laughed to June. "But you know it is very interesting to read these dog books and reflect back on child rearing."

To achieve a desired outcome, both parents and dog trainers need to be persistent as well as consistent in demanding a behavior and outcome. Rewarding good behavior by treats and praise promotes better and faster progress. Punishing bad behavior does not achieve the same magnitude of desired outcome as positive reinforcement.

"I wish we had read these dog books before we had kids," I joked to June.

June suggested some criteria to narrow down the search. We decided we wanted a dog that wouldn't shed, and would be intelligent, energetic and gentle, with no inherited joint dysplasia, eye disease, heart disease, or diabetes.

Shaudi had preferred a Labrador or Golden Retriever, as some of his friends had them. Neither breed met our criteria. While we were exhausting our brain cells on the "ideal" dog, a family friend, Joe, called us one day to declare with excitement that his family had acquired a Goldendoodle.

"A Goldendoodle! What is that?" I was excited too.

"It is a hybrid Golden Retriever and Poodle. The size of the 'doodle depends on the size of the poodle used for the breeding. There is a 60% chance a 'doodle will grow up like a poodle – intelligent, without hair shedding – and a 60% chance the doodle will inherit the retriever's gentle, friendly and energetic traits," Joe sounded like an expert although he hadn't read any dog books and we knew he was an impulsive consumer. Further, the numbers did not add well to a 100.

June and I researched it, and, indeed, the Goldendoodle was our "ideal" dog. We called up the same breeder Joe had used in eastern Washington State. The breeder told us Goldendoodles are becoming very popular and she had only two of the eight in the current litter still unclaimed. She could bring a puppy to us in four weeks, as she was coming our way to fly the other puppies to Texas and Korea.

During one July weekend, we went to the breeder to choose a puppy. She showed us the puppies and we were hooked. The furry little things were only two weeks old and so adorable. They played with each other with their little claws and bit each other with their little mouths. We could not leave the dog house. The breeder took the two unclaimed puppies out of the den. They continued to play in the open space. When they became bored, one walked away from us toward the door, and the smaller one crawled toward us. She was sociable and playful with Shaudi and she licked Lauda's hand.

"We'll take this one," both Shaudi and Lauda said.

June and I agreed. We paid a deposit and the breeder ink-marked the puppy's hair for us. We left the dog house later that afternoon feeling excited.

While it was easy for Shaudi and Lauda to choose the puppy, it meant a lot more work ahead for June and me. From our reading on dogs, we knew we had to get all kinds of supplies for the puppy such as a crate, water and food bowls, a blanket, etc. Training the dog to urinate and defecate outside, or potty training in dog owner terms, would be an important step in the early part of the puppy's life. Once she formed a bad habit, it would be hard to correct. We also needed to give her a name. I stayed quiet for several days, which was a signal I had something important on my mind. One day I said to June: "How about we name the new puppy Lisi? It's a Chinese name, but easy to pronounce in English."

"Li" means going away; "Si" means thinking of or missing someone. The name fit our context and occasion perfectly. My family unanimously accepted the name. The breeder called us two weeks later to confirm a delivery date. We had a month to prepare all the supplies to welcome Lisi when she arrived at 8 weeks old.

Outside training was the first order of business. Armed with knowledge learned from the dog books, June and I crafted a strict plan for feeding, play, and potty. We posted a schedule on the wall so everyone in the family knew what Lisi should be doing at any given time of the day. The first few nights were difficult, as she was distressed from separating from her companions. When left alone in her crate, Lisi would whine the whole night. She would be quiet during the daytime when someone was at home to pay attention to her. I took a week off to do the training. I would take Lisi out to potty at the same spot in the backyard after each feeding and every two hours during the daytime. I stretched the time interval by an hour each day. If she did her business, she would be allowed to play outside of her crate. Otherwise, she would be put back in the crate. She ate and drank inside the crate, so the crate was "her space" that she would not soil. This activity was recorded on the schedule, too, so everyone knew what had happened during the previous hours. June stayed up for the first several nights to help with the training. Amazingly, Lisi adapted quickly and didn't have any accidents in the house. Shaudi played happily with the puppy during daytime after school. He left Lisi to his parents to do the feeding, training, and cleaning up.

By the time Lisi was three months old, she needed more vaccination shots and a well-dog check up at the vet's office. When we called for an appointment, the lady at the registration desk asked what Lisi's last name was.

We were startled by this question.

"She is a dog. Does she need a family name?" June asked the receptionist.

"Yes, she does. She also needs a name tag with her home phone number on it," the woman said.

"We do not know her family name," June stammered. "She is from a large family in eastern Washington."

"Since you adopted her, she should adopt your family name!" the receptionist replied.

June and I laughed at this proposition and agreed to share our family name with Lisi.

We quickly enrolled Lisi Jiang in a behavioral training class at our local pet food store. The one-hour session was every Saturday morning. Initially, many puppies showed up, but, as the weeks went on, they dropped out quickly. The instructor frequently referred to June as Lisi's "mommy" and to me as Lisi' "daddy." We were again taken by this reference. I said to June, "We are the mama and papa of a dog. That is so funny. It would be a humiliation or insult to us in the Chinese culture to raise a dog's status to ours or reduce our status to the level of a dog."

June pointed out this was a true reflection on how human the American culture is.

"After all, the dog is a part of the family now," she said.

We adapted to this part of American culture quickly. We referred to Lisi as our child at home. We praised her by saying "good girl." We said, "Come to Mommy," or "Come to Daddy" when we called her to play with us.

By the sixth week of her classes, Lisi was the only dog at the graduation ceremony. Our parenting hadn't changed from Lauda and Shaudi's upbringings. We realized the doggy class was really to train the owners how to handle and train the dog at home. We practiced tricks we learned in class, such as "sit," "up," and "roll over," and we trained Lisi to respond to clickers and whistles. It was just like the children's homework. But we were a lot more lenient on Lisi than we ever were on Lauda or Shaudi. We cheered when Lisi was able to roll, a maneuver never used later. But we would not cheer if Lauda or Shaudi brought home a grade of A-.

In just a few months, Lisi's size had almost doubled. We allowed her more play time outside of her crate, yet, she did not want to go into the crate when we weren't home or when it was nighttime. We felt sorry for her, so we blocked each end of a hallway with a gate and let her stay there. She was teething, though, and she bit at the walls and the gates. So, I went into the garage and built a large den out of chicken wire to give her even more space. Soon, she tore up the wood frame. Eventually, Lisi was allowed free roam in the family room. Shaudi would play with her after school and periodically brush her teeth with dog toothpaste. June and I did all the walking, bathing and cleaning. Once Shaudi left for college, Lisi totally became June's and my responsibility.

Lisi has been a good dog. I used to notice that Lisi was the only one who welcomes me home every day after work. She frequently stayed at home alone for a whole day without causing any problem. The horror stories we had read and heard about, such as destroying furniture, sofas or pillows, were not conceivable with her. But we did have to be careful not to drop any metal paper clips, otherwise she would swallow them. She has made us go out walking or hiking a lot more frequently than we would otherwise do to prevent her (and us, too) gain much weight. She may also have served as an un-intended recipe for preventing our "empty-nest syndrome". I highly recommend other parents try getting a puppy when kids are getting out of home to college. In fact, I had recommended getting a puppy to several of my patients with good anti-depression and anti-anxiety effects. Shaudi once commented that Lisi helped him get the high score in his SAT-Biology when we probed him on how he did it without taking the class in high school.

> *Tip: "Dog is the best friend of man"; having a dog can ease family tension during college application, soothe your student's stress and may improve your student's academic performance.*

Lisi was "nosy" too. She "inspected" by sniffing every new shopping bag brought into the house. She knew all the goodies June shopped for the college-bound students.

13.3. The shopping list

Lauda was moving to California for college, so June headed to the mall. She was more excited than the student himself. June had devoted all her energies to raising our children, and, with our first having gained college admission, she felt the gratification of fine achievement. She wanted to pack him up well for the road and for campus life away from home. June prepared a long list of things to buy for Lauda months before college started. To accommodate the sizes of various students, the bed in the dormitory was eight feet long. Regular bed sheets would not work, so June searched for the extra-long size in the store's college bedding section. A duck-down cover and pillows naturally followed. Then, she calculated that, as Lauda was not likely be do his laundry every week, he would need 30 pairs of socks, 30 pieces of underwear, 10 t-shirts, and 7 pants, 7 shirts, and 7 coats. He would also need a bucket for taking his shampoo, soap, shaving cream, razor, toothpaste, and hairbrush to the shower; a laundry bag; a box of pre-packed, single-load laundry detergent; a file case for loose papers and homework assignments; a pair of shoes for sports; a pair of shoes for daily use; a pair of shoes for formal events; and yet another pair of shoes for use in the dorm. These were all "necessary" items on the shopping list. Then came school supplies: notebooks, a laptop computer and lock, a printer, printer paper, a box of pencils, and a carton of ballpoint pens.

"A refrigerator in the dormitory would be nice, as the weather will be so hot in California," June reasoned, adding a small fridge to the load. "Oh, and he will also need a desktop fan and clothes hangers."

She checked off most of the items on the list by the end of July – almost two months before Lauda was scheduled to start college.

Five years later, when we paid the deposit for Shaudi to attend Pomona College, I suggested June use Lauda's shopping list for Shaudi.

"No, I didn't keep that list," she said. "But, I don't need to make a shopping list for Shaudi. I received a list from the Pomona Parent Association last week."

"Social civilization has progressed a lot in five years," I said, shaking my head with disbelief when I saw the booklet "47 Things Every New Pomona Parent Needs to Know," prepared by the Experienced Parents of the Pomona Parents Association.

I read the title page aloud, "You and your child are in for the experience of a lifetime. From seasoned and savvy Pomona Parents, here are 47 tips to get ready for the next four years." Tip 1 was, "Ship after your shop. The mail room accepts boxes two weeks before Move-In-Day." The chapter went on for multiple pages.

I continued to read, stopping at tip 25.

"Look at this one," I said to June. "'Tip 25: Shop till you drop. Desktop fans, floor fan, flip-flops, spare toothbrush, desk lamp, are just some of the many things highly recommended.'"

I looked at my wife.

"The children here are really lucky," I said.

June had been paying attention to newspaper advertisements, hoping for some back-to-school sales. In those pages, she saw some stores offering a brilliant commercial idea: "The college dormitory bedding package." June was amazed to see the package was college-specific, as amenities in dorm rooms varied: some had walk-in closets, while others had a wardrobe in the room. I intrigued to see even more commercial ideas: a laundry package, a bath and shower package, and a study package.

It did not take long for June to stuff three suitcases with Shaudi's college "needs." But, she planned to purchase more.

"Since the airline charge fees for checked-in luggage, we will buy some items online and ship them to Shaudi's mail room as Tip 1 suggested and 'shop till we drop' for the rest once we are there, as Tip 25 recommended," June said.

> *Tip: Enjoy the chance to buy the things your soon-to-be collegian will need or want at school.*

Shaudi paid no attention to the growing pile of luggage, nor did he have any clue what he would need away from home. He didn't notice what June brought home from her frequent shopping expeditions. He was busy socializing with high school classmates and friends during the summer. His cell phone bill was high, since he was charged for texting over the limit. He took a biology class at the local community college and, to his credit, found a tutoring job at a Kumon school. Sometimes, I went to Shaudi's bedroom before going to work in the morning to see if Shaudi still existed, as I might not see him for days at a time.

"Shaudi is already practicing college student life: come home to sleep at midnight and not get up until noon, and he is out with friends before dinner time," I commented to June.

"I guess he will not suffer being homesick when he goes to college as I did," June answered.

13.4. Moving-in day on campus

On Friday, August 19th, 2011, everyone in our house got up at 5 a.m. I drove June and Shaudi to the airport to catch the 7 a.m. flight to Pomona College. I had loaded the luggage into the SUV the night before. After the two-hour flight, June rented a

169

car and off they went to the campus for a dry run and to check out the parking spaces. We had been there a few times previously for college campus visits. The street and the setting of the campus were still familiar. Shaudi saw the student who had greeted him at the train station and hosted him the night Shaudi visited the campus, before he decided on which college to attend. Dorm rooms were not officially open to new students, but building assignments had been released online, so Shaudi and June knew which building to check out. They easily sneaked into the building and previewed the room size and layout. Then, June and Shaudi went to local stores and took the advice of Tip 25: Shop till you drop. June had originally rented a Toyota Corolla sedan.

"This was obviously not a very 'practical car' for sending kids to college," June noted with regret in the parking lot. She managed to get a free upgrade to a station wagon.

Tip: For moving-in day, use or rent a large enough car to handle the load from shopping.

Saturday was the official moving-in day. Lauda had flown in the night before from Texas, where he was visiting friends, to join June and Shaudi at their hotel near Pomona. June drove herself and our sons in the fully loaded wagon from the hotel parking lot toward the campus. They chatted as she steered the car along familiar roads lined with well-pruned trees. It was a bright, sunny sky. There was a free breakfast and luncheon for everyone on campus. The temperature was in the high two-digit range. Sponsor students (upperclassmen) helped new students unload their luggage and find their assigned rooms. June and Lauda received a parent orientation schedule, while Shaudi joined the student orientation program. The parents' program ended at 5 p.m., with a "last check-in with your student." June had read that there would be many quiet rooms in the common area with a plenty of tissues for parents. She located these rooms and checked the supplies in case of need. But, Lauda's companionship had helped make this unnecessary for her.

I stayed at home, continually monitoring my family's progress in California via cell phone and texting technology.

"Should Shaudi buy the 14- or 21-meal plan per week?" June asked me.

"The 14-meal plan means he will only eat two meals per day. That may not be enough. Do they offer a 19-meal program? This way, he can eat three meals during the week and sleep in during the weekend with two meals per day," I said.

I was inventing a program, making me of limited use to June as she tried to make decisions quickly.

"Lauda did the 14-meal plan and set up a flexible account for extra food, if needed, at other food stores," June said. "Shaudi can change the meal plan to fit his desire after a few weeks of living here."

As always, June's logic was impeccable.

I had told June I couldn't go with her and Lauda to send Shaudi off because "I have to stay home to work for the tuitions."

Some of our family friends joked that I was afraid of separation anxiety and might become too emotional when the time came to leave the campus. That's what had happened five years before when I left Lauda on campus and drove home alone. That time, it had been just Lauda and me. I had enlarged the cargo area of our SUV by folding down the back seats, but there still wasn't enough space for Lauda's moving-to-campus gear for Stanford. I took his mountain bike apart to fit it into the gaps, and I moved the 2-cubic foot refrigerator out of its packing box to save precious space. Finally, Lauda and I were on our way, driving to California at 7 a.m., on a Saturday in September. Lauda was a fully licensed and mature driver by then, after having driven to school by himself for two years during high school. He was a great help to relieve me from driving fatigue. We took a few breaks on the road to rest and eat. It took us 12 hours of driving to reach campus by 9 p.m. We checked into a nearby hotel for the night. Too soon on that Sunday morning, the California day broke with beaming sun rays. By the time we got to campus, it was busy with vans, trucks and cars, as well as new students and their family members. Upperclassmen stood in front of each dormitory to help the newcomers and to give out the program for moving-in day.

The dormitory room was intended for four freshman students. The room was further divided into 3 sections. The two end sections functioned like a private room. Each had a space for a bed and desk with a doorway leading to the larger in-between section which had two beds and two desks. Upon arrival at the dormitory, we found one of the "private rooms" had been taken by an athlete student who had arrived 3 weeks earlier to practice football; the other "private room" was taken by a student who lived nearby the campus and had brothers and sisters attended the same university and knew the tricks of "first come, first grab". In the larger section the bed near the window and away from the doorway already had bedding on it. The left over bed was next to the doorway against the back wall without a window. As we were the last arrived at the dormitory, the left over bed became Lauda's sleeping spot for the first year.

Tip: To get the best location of the bed, arrive early at the dormitory: all colleges have the policy of "first come, first grab"

After helping Lauda make his bed, hang his clothes in a wardrobe, set up his desk fan, plug in his lamp, and assemble a plastic dresser, I wanted to say something to Lauda but found I could not. I felt myself welling up, my eyes watering. Lauda's eyes got redder and redder. I quickly left the dorm room, no hugging or good-bye or looking back. I wanted to avoid a full-out emotional breakdown in front of Lauda and other students. I went to the parents' program, which was hosted by the provost, while Lauda joined other freshmen for the student orientation.

At 4 p.m., the parent group broke up, and parents were supposed to leave campus. I stood on a corner of the street and watched Lauda and a group of his new friends talking in the front yard of the dorm building. I don't know how long I stood there. I knew Lauda sensed my presence, but we tried to avoid eye contact with each other. Finally, the students were led inside the building. Lauda disappeared in the hallway. I slowly got back into the SUV. I intended to leave the campus and head out for the long drive home. Once in the car, my self-control and my guard broke. I folded my head into my arms against the steering wheel. My whole body shook. I had never had such a profound, total loss-of-control, howling cry in my life. After what felt like an eternity, I said to myself, "Peter, you need to get going for the long drive." I collected myself and drove several circles around the dorm building hoping, without success, to have one more peek at Lauda.

Tip: Your emotions may surprise you on move-in day.
Let them flow.

The Sunday afternoon drive on California 101 was not as bad as the weekdays, and the September sun was still high at 7 p.m. With an empty car trunk, I was able to speed toward the east. My emotions were up and down the whole way. Frequently, I broke down in tears. I finally became sober when I reached

Sacramento. I called June at home. I asked her to bid on a hotel from Priceline.com for me for that night, in Redding, a small city in northern California. I reflected as I waited for her to tell me the results of the bid. After all, my emotional breakdown felt very strange and I had no rational explanation. Was it from pride in successful parenting? Was it my son's success in getting into a top college? Was it the sadness of separation, the severing of the father-son bond? Or was I jealous of the luck Lauda enjoyed? My own trip to college in China had been very different.

After the college entrance exam at my high school in May 1981, all students were dismissed to go back to their homes in their villages. The summer before starting college was no different than any of my previous summer breaks. I read a lot and finished all the Chinese classical novels, including the *Red Tower Dream* and *The Evolution of 3 Nations*, in my spare time after completing work on the farm. There was no electric light. I read mainly at night under an oil lamp made from a soaked strip of cloth hung over a used ink bottle filled with diesel oil. By morning, my nasal cavities would be filled with black tar. I socialized with a half-dozen students from nearby villages who attended the same high school and all were eagerly awaiting news. After a month at home, the test scores came out and all students went back to our high school to select colleges. Our guiding principle was not which "dream college" we wanted to attend, rather, it was which college most likely accept us based on our test scores. For students with my background, the only reason to study was to get into a college and get out of the countryside with the lowest social economic condition at that time in the world by any measurement. We hoped to live in the city after college, and be like those workers in the tall buildings. We did not dare to dream to become a doctor or an engineer or a professor or a government official. It was too unrealistic. There was no family member or relative example to follow. In those years, the Teacher's College and the Medical College were the two most unpopular college categories, thus easier to get in. Because of their lack of appeal, these unpopular schools were granted priority right to pick students ahead of the other colleges. For my first choice, I selected an Engineering College, to major in physics. For my second choice, I selected the Medical College. My third choice was the Teacher's College. My test scores were good enough for all three colleges. When the Engineering College looked for my file, the Medical College had taken my file three days before. My future life was thus determined: Medical College. I later learned from the admissions officer who picked up my file that she liked my leadership role in my high school class.

I was admitted to college.

Life continued as usual. There was no celebration and no shopping. The winter would be much colder in northern China, where I was going. My mother filled a jacket and shoes with cotton to help keep me warm. She re-worked my high school quilt with more cotton filling. My luggage was one bed sheet, folded and tied by its four corners. It probably weighed about ten pounds. The faded, green school bag my sister had used in high school was washed clean and filled with papers and dry food for the road. My mother stayed at home and my father went with me to Baofeng. We stayed a night at my aunt's home so we could catch a passing train the next morning. I had never been to a city or ridden on a train. The farthest place from home I had been was high school. There was no separation anxiety or fear, though, as I had been away from home for school for the past three years and did not know what would be coming to me.

We bought a train ticket through a relative who worked at the train station. With the ticket in my hand and the bulky, folded sheet-luggage on my back, and the school bag at my side, I bid goodbye to my father, my aunt's husband, and the relative who secured the ticket. I did not cry, nor did I see my father or mother break down, just as Lauda would not see me become emotional decades later.

Upon boarding the train, I immediately encountered a huge crowd. Passengers were standing in the hallway or sitting on the floor. There was no way to move. My luggage clung to my back like the shell of a tortoise. I was stuck at the train car's entrance. It would be a 15-hour train ride without a place to sit or to rest my luggage. I was hoping I could move closer to the bathroom when passengers came off the train along the way. But the bathroom proved not necessary, as I had only dry food to eat and no water. I arrived at the Beijing train station early the next morning. I used the bathroom there and asked how to get onto the next train to Tangshan. My parents had not been able to explain how to ride trains, since neither of them had ever been on a train. I was directed to a long line snaking around the opening of the station. There was a little, dark window open to the waiting travelers. There were hundreds of people congregated; all passengers heading to northeastern China had to line up for that little dark window.

"Why are people lined up here?" I asked an elderly person standing next to me.

"You have to get a transfer ticket from the person on the other side of the little window to board the train to your next destination. Where are you going and when is your next train, youngster?" the man asked.

"I am going to Tangshan for college, and I do not know when the next train is," I answered.

"By the way your accent sounds, you're from Henan Province. I'm from Henan Province too. We are hometown fellows. I have lost my wallet and money. Can you spare some money so I can buy a ticket home? I'll mail the money back to you and write a letter to your college to praise your generosity," the older man became much friendlier to me.

I told the man I had only 30 yuan. It equaled $3 then and it equals $5 now.

"I can only give you 10 yuan. I need the 20 yuan for my first month's food at college," I said. I was innocently honest.

The man took the money and quickly left the line and disappeared into the massive crowds. I did not know I had been scammed. It was my first real trip away from home.

I patiently stayed in the line and, little by little, moved forward. There were frequent line jumpers, which made the line move even slower. I had the bulky baggage on my back and I was constantly reminded by the loud overhead speaker never to leave the luggage unattended or ask someone else to look after it. I could not jump the line even if I wanted to, as this required physical pushing. It was another 12 hours of standing and nibbling on dry food. By mid-afternoon, I was finally at the little window.

"I am going to Tangshan," I shouted at the window, so as to be heard over the noise in the station.

"Next available train departs at 9 p.m.," the lady inside said emotionlessly. She pasted a sticker onto my original ticket.

I was relieved. But, as I moved a few steps away from the line, a dizzy sensation rushed to my head. I had not eaten a meal, drunk any water, or slept for 32 hours. I sat on the floor and untied the luggage from my shoulder and placed it on the floor. I laid on the concrete floor for a nap.

"Wake up. Move away," a member of the evening cleaning crew shouted. He was in a hurry to finish the last wipe of the floor before going home.

I had slept for three hours on the cool floor and awoke with dreams still sifting through my thoughts. I vividly remembered attending a wedding event at home with tables and tables full of food, but I was not allowed to touch any of it. In another dream, I was jumping in the little lake a mile south from my home in the village to catch a big fish. I had done this many times. But, in the dream, I could not move my arms to swim. I was drowning and I could not breathe.

"Oh. Thank you for rescuing me," I said to the cleaning person.

He did not pay any attention to me, a shabby country boy.
I went to the station's bathroom area. People were brushing their teeth and washing their faces with cold water. They had brought cups to collect boiling water to drink from a tank in the corner of the bathroom area. I did not have a cup for hot water. I saw no one swallow the cold water.

"Is this water drinkable?" I asked a person near the sink.

"No. You will get diarrhea," the person said.

I had no choice. I was severely dehydrated. Forming my hands into a scoop, I swallowed many scoops of the washing water. Feeling refreshed, I looked for the boarding platform. Fortunately, the next train originated from the Beijing station and I had a seat for the seven-hour ride. I rationed my bag of dry food for the last leg of the trip. By 4 a.m., the fourth day since I left home, I was at my destination and was greeted by students from the Medical College.

"Where is your luggage?" a senior class student asked.

"This is it. Do you have any water?" I replied.

I climbed into the open bed of a truck skillfully and indulged in the water provided by the senior classman. A short ride later, the senior classman lead me to the dorm room.

"This is your room and I live in the next building," he said. "Let me know if you need any help."

There were three, metal-frame bunk beds intended for six students. One bed already had bedding on it. I picked a lower-level bed next to a window facing southeast. I untied the sheet holding my belongings and spread my things on the bed. The bed was much better quality than what I was used to sleeping on in high school. This bed had a nicely knitted rice straw mattress on top of wooden slats. It was fairly soft and, for me, it had a nostalgic straw smell. I was long since ready to indulge in this nice bed. I rolled the cotton-filled jacket my mother made into a pillow. I covered myself with the cotton quilt. I was officially "moved in" at college. I fell asleep in a second and started new dreams from that moment on.

Years later, as I sat, lost in thought in Redding, California, waiting for my wife to tell me the result of her Priceline.com hotel bid, I was not sure what to make of my college move-in compared to Lauda's and Shaudi's. I was certainly gratified and proud that, through my hardship, my children did not have to go through what I did. To this day, I still cannot explain why I cried all the way to Sacramento. "I have a small tear sac and it easily spills," I joke. I would have most probably have stirred everyone's "tear sacs" had I gone to Shaudi's move-in day at Pomona College. It was wise for me to stay at home to "earn the tuition."

Tip: As you cram your car full of your student's belongings, be sure to keep a corner of your glove compartment open for a box of tissues for the parents."

Chapter 14. Facts and fictions on the value of college education

14.1.   The value of college education

Highly publicized studies show personal income later life correlates with an educational degree attained earlier in life. In many societies, higher education is also likely to bring ascendance in social class. Certainly, in some societies, a child's birth into a powerful or higher-class family guarantees a better career and life. For the vast majority of the population, though, hard work toward a higher education is the only path to a "revolution" in inherited social class. This "revolution" not only changes the current generation's life path, but it also changes future generations by allowing them to be born into a family with money and knowledge garnered through education. In some sense, in every society there exist opportunities, some more and some less, for its population to succeed. It is up to the wisdom of parents and the determination of their student to achieve the goal of a college degree.

My childhood experience serves as a good illustration of the importance of college education and hard work. My birth was in a remote, rural village. My mother never attended school and did not know how to read or count. My father had a high school diploma, which was rare for his generation, and he became an elementary and middle school teacher for village schools. But he never taught in the schools my siblings or I attended, nor did he teach us at home.

The day I started school was in the summer of 1970. I was 7 years old. It was morning, and I was playing with a neighbor's boy, Jianmin, at a pond outside of the village. We were throwing small rocks into the pond, competing to see who could make rocks skip more on the surface of the water. I extended my fist backward, holding a rock, in preparation for a forward thrust. I didn't realize Jianmin was close behind me. My fist hit Jianmin in the face. Jianmin hit me back. Soon, we were tangled together fighting. A schoolteacher happened to pass by. The teacher separated us and asked, "What are you two fighting for? Why aren't you in school?"

"We do not go to any school," I answered.

"What is your birth year animal?" the teacher asked.

I said, "I am rabbit"

Jianmin said, "I am tiger."

"Then, both of you should go to school. Follow me to start school today," the teacher commanded.

There was no preschool, no kindergarten, no school open house, no orientation, no registration, no school start kit. Jianmin was already one year late, as he was 8 years old.

I walked in to a classroom holding 25 students. Half were in first grade and half were in second grade. One teacher taught the two grades. Over the next few days, I learned how things worked. The teacher would instruct the second graders first, and then assign some in-class homework to keep them engaged. Then, the teacher's attention would shift to the first graders. The courses were mathematics and Chinese character writing practice. Using sticks to write on the dirt in the ground, students had to write each character 20 to 30 times. It was a good way to learn Chinese, as the characters indeed became engraved in the mind as the hand moved when writing a given character. Practice was similar for addition and subtraction in math class. At the end of each school day, there were tests. The teacher would randomly call students to the blackboard. The student would have to use chalk to write words or equations the teacher randomly picked from previous sessions. Students had to work on and know assignments well, otherwise they would be embarrassed in front of the whole class. There was no homework. In non-farming season, after-school activities were running around the village or playing hide-and-seek between barns. Still, many of students dropped out of school. For example, after two days in first grade, a girl from my class said, "I do not want to play with you anymore." She left class and never returned to school. Her parents had never attended school themselves, so they did not have the wisdom to force her to come back to school. The girl died of leukemia when I was in fifth grade.

Students in third and fourth grades also shared one classroom and teacher. Only fifth graders had the privilege of not sharing a classroom. In sixth grade, students from several nearby villages merged into one school in my village. There were about 80 students divided into two classes in the middle school, which shared a campus with the elementary school. There were more courses in middle school, including physics, chemistry, agriculture, and social politics. We still studied math and Chinese. I went to school because most kids I knew did. For me, there was no clear purpose for learning, yet. There was no hope of going to college – China was in the turmoil of the Cultural Revolution and all colleges were closed to merit-based enrollment. My grades were average. Once I became a teenager, I was frequently absent from class, as I was expected to help support my family. My father was teaching in other villages far away. He only came home for a weekend every few weeks. So, I had to spend more time working on the community farm to earn points to gain my family more grain allowance. There was no more hide-and-seek between barns after school. I would herd community oxen or cut grass along the riverbank to feed the oxen. My mother and sister also worked hard to earn points; my younger brothers were not yet expected to do so. During summer break, I would team with friends to dig and clean the riverbed to get better irrigation for autumn crops. Cleaning a 100-meter-long riverbed, four meters deep by four meters wide, earned our team 100 points. We friends would split the points equally. Since we were teenagers and full of energy, we could complete a project quickly.

My outside-of-school activities soon forced me to repeat sixth grade. My family was building a house, and I was expected to help adult workers transport wagons of rocks from remote mountains to the building site, then to help masons lay the bricks in a straight line. I missed too much school to progress with my class. In 1977, as I was attempting sixth grade for the second time, Deng Xiao Ping, the Chinese communist warrior, was back in power in the communist party. Colleges re-opened to students nationwide. The first group of college students were enrolled by academic merit or their college entrance test score. My father and other teachers brought this news to me at the school.

"But what can I do to get into college?" I asked.

"Study hard," was the answer.

By now, the new house was complete. It was larger than our previous house, and I had my own room. I gathered many old books from my father's collection, and, after attending regular school, I taught myself at night under an oil lamp. My friends played in barns, but, reading alone at night, my mind brightened with hope. The equations in the math and physics classes and the formula and reaction process in the chemistry class were all making sense. This newly found knowledge was enjoyable and exciting. My grades rose to the top in the class. Since I was also "senior" over the other students, I was well-respected by peers and liked by my teachers. I was elected class president. My father and an elderly uncle who was also a teacher frequently inquired about my grades and my class performance.

They were happy at my class presidency, explaining it signaled a well-rounded student. Every semester, I was voted the "good student" in three aspects: morality, intelligence, and fitness. I brought these "good student" certificates home, and, soon, the walls in the family home ran out of space for posting them. In 1978, the Baofeng high school re-opened its doors to students county-wide, with admission based on high school entrance test scores. Among the 80 graduating students in my seventh grade class in the village, I was the only one whose test scores led to my admission at Baofeng high school.

Most of my classmates who remained in the village became famers, just like the generations before them had been for several thousand years. On my annual visits to my mother and other relatives in the village, many of my elementary and middle school classmates come, and we sit and talk late into the night. They like tasting the foreign cigarettes I buy them at the duty free shop. Jianmin, my childhood friend, is a mason. He leads a commercial construction team that builds houses for the villagers. Another close friend raises chickens. Several others are dealers in coal products. These former classmates are still my friends, but the split in our educational experiences means we live a world apart, both by geography and by social status. Lauda and Shaudi witnessed this many times and were impressed by their father's close friendships with his classmates even after so many years had passed.

14.2. The goal of higher education

I often think about my childhood classmates. I reflect on the difference between my life experience and theirs. In terms of academics, the amount of my schooling and number of my degrees place me far above and beyond the sum of those attained by all my classmates combined. By international and national experience, the distance I have traveled is, again, more than all my classmates combined. So what was the difference of more education for me versus my classmates? By wealth, I am not at the top. The coal dealers have much larger bank accounts. Therefore, if monetary accumulation is the ultimate measurement of the value of education, the importance of education certainly would not attest to that argument for me. So what is the goal of higher education? Judging by personal health, there are no major illnesses among my classmates at this stage of life. Judging by fame, yes, I may attract more villagers to my home when I come to visit my family, but I also provide free healthcare advice when I am there. Judging by social status, yes, I may have connections who can be helpful in fulfilling certain desires. My classmates often ask me to activate these connections to do favors for them or for their offspring. Judging by happiness, all my childhood classmates seem quite content with their daily personal and family lives. So, why should I have gone for so much more schooling? Is it that more education yields a higher probability of success in society, and a better quality and standard of living? Or is it that more education provides a better chance for one to lead a life beyond materialistic gratification? The theoretical physicist Albert Einstein said: "Only a life lived for others is a life worthwhile." This philosophy supports my educational experience. I probably provide "more services" for others.

Following this theory, maybe the goal of a college education is to prepare a person for a better chance to lead a successful life. Then how to define success? The definition from *Webster's Dictionary and Thesaurus* is a "desired or favorable outcome." To expect an outcome, there should be a task to either successfully achieve or fail to achieve. A simple example is the task of a car repair. My car would not start one morning, so I drove off in June's car. June called a friend to come by to jumpstart the car. It worked. June then drove the car to the car shop, where the technician replaced the battery. I drove the car to work the next day. June successfully achieved the desired outcome for the task for me, via payment to the car shop technician. But, what is the task of life, or the purpose of life? What would be a desirable outcome for a life? Some people link success or a desirable outcome of life to the attainment of wealth, of eminence, and of power. When I discussed this topic at church, our pastor immediately renounced that concept. But, if a person does define a successful life as attaining wealth, fame, and influence, then what role does college education play? The next few sections explain my research-based presumptive conclusions (as the statistics are far from conclusive).

14.3. Twenty of the 400 richest Americans and the colleges they attended

Forbes Magazine publishes many lists, including ones ranking individual people's wealth. I looked at a *Forbes Magazine* from October 10, 2011, and researched the top ten and bottom ten billionaires on the list. I looked at their age at the time, their personal wealth, the college they attended for their undergraduate degrees, and the college's rank as listed by *US News & World Report* in 2012.

The top ten billionaires

Name	Profile	College	College rank
1. Bill Gates, age 55	Microsoft, $59B	Harvard University, MA (attended)	#1
2. Warren Buffett, age 81	Berkshire Hathaway, $39B	University of Pennsylvania's Wharton School and the University of Nebraska (attended both but graduated from UN).	#5 #101
3. Larry Ellison, age 67	Oracle, $33B	University of Illinois and the University of Chicago, IL (attended both).	#147 #5 (tight)
4. Charles Koch, age 75	Diversified, $25B	Massachusetts Institute of Technology	#5 (tight)
5. David Koch,	Diversified,	Massachusetts Institute	#5

age 71	$25B	of Technology	
6. Christy Walton, age 56 (wife of deceased John Walton)*	Wal-Mart, $24.5B	*College* of Wooster, OH (for John Walton)	#71
7. George Soros, age 81	Hedge Funds, $22B	University of Toronto, Canada	n/a (not ranked)
8. Sheldon Adelson, age 81	Casinos, $21.5B	City College of NY (attended)	n/a (not ranked)
9. Jim Walton, age 63	Wal-Mart, $21.1B	University of Arkansas	#132
10. Alice Walton, age 61	Wal-Mart, $20.9B	Trinity College in San Antonio, TX	Regional #1**

*Christy Walton retained the wealth after John Walton died.

**Regional ranking: as opposed to national colleges, regional colleges are considered 2nd tier in the ranking category.

The bottom ten billionaires

Name	Profile	College	College rank
391. Patrick G. Ryan, age 74	Insurance, $1.1B	Northwestern University, IL	#12
392. Bernard Francis Saul II, age 79	Banking, real estate, $1.1B	Villanova University, PA	Regional #1*
393. Alexander Spanos, age 87	Real estate, $1.1B	University of the Pacific, CA	#101
394. Mark Stevens, age 51	Venture capital, $1.1B	University of Southern California, CA	#23
395. Jon Stryker, age 53	Medical technology, $1.1B	Kalamazoo College, MI	#68

396. Jerry Yang, age 42	Yahoo, $1.1B	Stanford University, CA	#5 (tight)
397. Darwin Deason, age 71	Xerox, $1.05B	None	n/a
398. Peter Lewis, age 77	Progressive Co, $1.05B	Princeton University, NJ	#1 (tight)
399. Steven Roth, age 69	Real estate, $1.05B	Dartmouth University, NH	#11
400. Daniel M. Snyder, age 46	Red Zone Capital, $1.05B	University of Maryland (attended)	#58

*Regional ranking: as opposed to national colleges, regional colleges are considered 2nd tier in the ranking category.

Analysis:

Of the 20 richest Americans analyzed:

- Half (10) attended or graduated from one of the top 50 colleges
- 15% (three) attended or graduated from a college ranked from 51st-100th
- 20% (four) attended or graduated from a college ranked from 100th to 150th
- 25% (five) attended or graduated from a college ranked beyond 151st.

Some of the people count more than once, as they attended more than one colleges.

Presumptive conclusion: Attending the top ranked 50 colleges seems to help a student in joining the super-rich club.

14.4. The most powerful 30 U.S. political leaders and the colleges they attended

But not all people are drawn to wealth. If the leader of a country is the most powerful person in that country, then the ten most recent American presidents would be the ten most powerful people in America, even if their tenures never overlap. Every one of them holds a college degree. Ranks, again, are from the 2012 *US News & World Report* college analysis.

The 10 most recent US Presidents

Name	Profile	College	College rank
Barack Obama	44th President: 2009-present	Occidental College, CA 1981 (attended)	#37
		Columbia University, NY, 1983 (graduated)	#4
George W. Bush	43rd President: 2001-2009	Yale University, CT, 1968	#3
William Clinton	42nd President: 1993-2001	Georgetown University, DC, 1968	#22
George H.W. Bush	41st President 1989-1993	Yale University, CT, 1948	#3
Ronald Reagan	40th President: 1981-1989	Eureka College, IL, 1932	Regional #40
James Carter	39th President: 1977-1981	Naval Academy, MD, 1946	#14
Gerald Ford	38th President: 1974-1977	University of Michigan, MI, 1935	#28
Richard Nixon	37th President: 1969-1974	Whittier College, CA, 1934	#133
Lyndon Johnson	36th President: 1963-1969	Texas State University-San Marcos, 1930	Regional #39*
John Kennedy	35th President: 1961-1963	Harvard University, MA, 1940	#1

*Regional ranking: as opposed to national colleges, regional colleges are considered 2nd tier in the ranking category.

Analysis:

Of the last 10 US Presidents:

- 70% (seven) attended or graduated from one of the top 50 colleges;
- none (0) attended or graduated from a college ranked from 51st-100th
- 10% (one) attended or graduated from a college ranked from 100th to 150th
- 20% (two) attended or graduated from a college ranked beyond 151st.

Presumptive conclusion (as this statistic is far from conclusive): Attending top ranked 50 colleges seems to give a student a much better chance to become a US President.

But not all people are drawn to the ultimate in power. Some people want to be leaders, but of a segment of the government, not the entire government. This would be party leaders, both in the US Senate and US House of Representatives. Ranks, again, are from the 2012 *US News & World Report* college analysis.

The ten most recent party leaders in the US Senate

Name	Profile	College	College rank
Harry Reid (NV)	Dem (Majority), 2005-present	Utah State University	#171
Mitch McConnell (KY)	Rep, (minority) 2007- present	University of Louisville, KY, 1964	#164
Tom Daschle (SD)	Dem (m/M), 1995-2005	South Dakota State University, 1969	#194
Bill Frist (TN)	Rep (M) 2003-	Princeton University,	#1

	2007	NJ, 1974	
Trent Lott (MS)	Rep (M/m) 1996-2003	University of Mississippi, MS, 1963	#143
George Mitchell (ME)	Dem (M), 1989-1995	Bowdoin College, ME, 1954	#6
Robert Dole (KS)	Rep (M/m) 1985-1996	University of Kansas, 1945	#101
Robert Byrd (WV)	Dem (m/M) 1977-1989	Marshall University, WV, 1994 (graduated with a Bachelor degree)	Regional #39*
Howard Baker (TN)	Rep (m/M) 1977-1985	Tulane University, LA, 1943	#50
Mike Mansfield (MT)	Dem (M) 1961-1977	University of Montano, MT, 1934	#194

*Regional ranking: as opposed to national colleges, regional colleges are considered 2nd tier in the ranking category.

The ten most recent Speakers of the US House of Representative

Name	Profile	College	College rank
John Boehner (Oh)	Rep, 2011-present	Xavier University, OH, 1977	Regional #4*
Nancy Pelosi (CA)	Dem, 2007- 2011	Trinity Washington University, DC, 1962	Regional #250*
Dennis Hastert (IL)	Rep, 1999-2007	Wheaton College, IL, 1964	#57
Newt Gingrich (GA)	Rep, 1995-1999	Emory University, GA, 1965	#20
Tom Foley (WA)	Dem, 1989-2003	University of Washington, 1951	#42
Jim Wright	Dem, 1987-1989	Weatherford	n/a

(TX)		University, TX; University of Texas, Austin	#45
Tip O'Neil (MA)	Dem, 1977-1987	Boston College, MA, 1936	#53
Carl Albert (OK)	Dem, 1971-1977	University of Oklahoma, 1931	#101
John McCormack (MA)	Dem, 1962-1971	none	
Sam Rayburn (TX)	Dem, 1955-1961	Texas A&M University, 1903	#58

*Regional ranking: as opposed to national colleges, regional colleges are considered 2nd tier in the ranking category.

Analysis:

Of the 20 analyzed US Congressional leaders:

- 30% (six) attended or graduated from one of the top 50 colleges;
- 15% (three) attended or graduated from a college ranked from 51st-100th;
- 15% (three) attended or graduated from a college ranked from 100th to 150th;
- 40% (eight) attended or graduated from a college ranked beyond 151st.

Presumptive conclusion: To become a leader in the US politics, any college education is fine. There seems no need to carry heavy tuition debt from the expensive colleges.

14.5. The 10 most influential Americans and the colleges they attended

In a vastly complicated world, it is highly debatable who is the most influential person. Even the person selected for the annual cover of *Time* magazine's "Most Influential People" edition does not receive universal approval. But, for the purpose of this section, the work of the *Time* editors provides the best material. There are other nationalities in this rank besides Americans. Since this book focuses on American colleges and universities, I chose to analyze 10 Americans, as of year 2012, with an American college degree. Again, college rankings are from the list provided by the 2012 *US News & World Report*.

Name	Profile	College	College rank
Mark Zuckerberg	2010, Founder, Facebook	Harvard University, MA (attended for two years)	#1
Ben Bernanke	2009, Chairman, Federal Reserve	Princeton University, NJ	#1 (tight)
Barack Obama	2008 and 2012, the 44th US President	Occidental College, CA 1981 (attended) Columbia University, NY, 1983	#37 #4
Bill Gates	2005, Founder, Microsoft	Harvard University, MA (attended)	#1
George W. Bush	2004, the 42nd US President	Yale University, CT, 1968	#3
Rudolph Giuliani	2001, former Mayor, New York City	Manhattan College, NY, 1965	Regional #15*
Jeff Bezos	1999, Founder, Amazon.com	Princeton University, NJ, 1986	#1
Bill Clinton	1998, 41st US President	Georgetown University, 1968	#22
David Ho	1996, Scientist, AIDS research	California Institute of Technology, CA, 1974	#5

| Newt Gingrich | 1995 former speaker, US House of Representatives | Emory University, GA, 1965 | #20 |

*Regional ranking: as opposed to national colleges, regional colleges are considered 2nd tier in the ranking category.

Analysis:

Of the 10 most influential Americans, 90% (nine) attended or graduated from one of the top 50 colleges.

Presumptive conclusion: Attending top ranked 50 colleges appears to give a student a much better chance to influence America on a grand scale.

14.6. The ten most recent American Nobel Laureates in science/economy and the colleges they attended.

Not everyone deems politicians or billionaires to be the greatest contributors to society. In that case, the scientists who earned a Nobel Prize should be respected for their talents and gifts to humanity. Again, only Nobel Laureates with an American college degree are listed here. The 10 most recent as of 2012 are in the table, with their college assigned its 2012 ranking from *US News & World Report*.

Name/affiliation	Profile	College	College rank
Saul Perlmutter at University of California-Berkeley	2011, Physics, "for the discovery of accelerating universe"	Harvard University	#1
Brian Schmidt at Australian National University,	2011, Physics, "for the discovery of accelerating universe"	University of Arizona, 1989	#124

Australia			
Adam Riess at Johns Hopkins University	2011, Physics, "for the discovery of accelerating universe"	Massachusetts Institute of Technology, 1992	#5
Bruce Beutler at Scripps Research Institute, CA, University of Texas Southwestern Medical Center at Dallas	2011, Medicine, "for … discoveries concerning the activation of innate immunity"	University of California-San Diego, 1976	#37
Thomas Sargent at New York University	2011, Economic Science, "for … empirical research on cause and effect in the macroeconomy"	University of California-Berkeley	#21
Christopher Sims at the Princeton University	2011, Economic Science, "for … empirical research on cause and effect in the macroeconomy"	Harvard University, 1963	#1
Peter Diamond at the Massachusetts Institute of Technology	2010, Economic Science, "for their analysis of markets with search frictions"	Yale University, 1960	#3
Dale T Mortensen at Northwestern University-Evanston	2010, Economic Science, "for their analysis of markets with search frictions"	Willamette University, OR, 1961	#57
Richard F. Heck at the University of Delaware	2010, Chemistry, "for palladium-catalyzed cross couplings in organic synthesis"	University of California-Los Angeles, 1952	#25

Carol W. Greider at Johns Hopkins University	2009, Medicine, "for palladium-catalyzed cross couplings in organic synthesis"	University of California-Santa Barbara, 1983	#42

Analysis: Of the 10 Nobel Laureates with an American college degree, 80% (eight) attended or graduated from one of the top 50 colleges.

Presumptive conclusion: Attending top ranked 50 colleges appears to give a student a much needed education to advance in science.

14.7. The top oncologists in the greater Seattle area and the undergraduate colleges they attended

Since I am a medical oncologist, I naturally have the highest regard for colleagues in this field. I include here the "2012 'Top Docs' in Medical Oncology" published by *Seattle Magazine* (www.seattlemag.com July 2012, page 108). I took out my own name, as I do not have an American college degree. Also not posted here but on the original list are Drs. Stephen Chen (with degrees from China) and Joachim Deeg (with degrees from Germany). Colleges, as before, are assigned their 2012 ranking from *US News & World Report*.

Name	Profile	College for undergraduate	College rank
David Aboulafia	Virginia Mason Medical Center	University of Michigan, 1975	#28
Frederick Appelbaum	Fred Hutchinson Cancer Research Center, University of Washington	Dartmouth University,1968	#11

Anthony Back	University of Washington	Stanford University, 1980	#5
Oliver Batson	The Everett Clinic	Brown University, 1980	#15
David Dong	Puget Sound Cancer Centers	UC Berkeley, 1980	#21
Philip Gold	Swedish Cancer Institute	Columbia University, 1987	#4
Douglass Lee	Puget Sound Cancer Centers	Harvard University, 1977	#1
David Maloney	Fred Hutchinson Cancer Research Center, University of Washington	Whitworth College, WA, 1977	Regional #9*
Malpass, Thomas W	Virginia Mason Medical Center	University of North Carolina, 1971	#29
Vincent Picozzi	Virginia Mason Medical Center	Yale University, 1974	#3
David White	The Polyclinic	?? (not available publically)	

*Regional ranking: as opposed to national colleges, regional colleges are considered 2nd tier in the ranking category.

Analysis: Of the 10 oncologists with available data, 90% (nine) attended and graduated from one of the top 50 colleges.

Presumptive conclusion: Attending one of the top-ranked 50 colleges appears to give a student a better chance to succeed in the field of cancer medicine.

14.8. The CEOs *Fortune's* 2011 top 500 American companies and the colleges they attended

An ambitious worker may aim to occupy the top executive suite at a large company. These are the 1% in society, envied or resented by the other 99%. They were the target of the "occupy" movement in 2011. These people can make the greatest difference in corporate America. *Fortune* magazine lists the top 500 companies every year. For the 2011, list, I looked at the undergraduate college education of the CEOs at the top 10 companies. Colleges, as before, are assigned their 2012 ranking from *US News & World Report*.

Name	Profile	Attended	College rank
1. Michael Duke	Wal-Mart Stores CEO since 2009	Georgia Institute of Technology, 1971	#36
2. Rex Tillerson	Exxon Mobil CEO since 2006	University of Texas-Austin, 1974	#45
3. John Watson	Chevron CEO since 2010	University of California-Davis, 1978	#38
4. James Mulva	ConocoPhillips CEO since 2002	University of Texas-El Paso, 1968	Not ranked
5. Michael Williams	Fannie Mae CEO since 2009	Drexel University, PA	#88
6. Jeffrey Immelt	General Electric CEO since 2001	Dartmouth University, NH, 1977	#11
7. Warren Buffett	Berkshire Hathaway CEO since 1970	University of Nebraska, OM, 1950	#101
8. Daniel Akerson	General Motors CEO since 2010	US Naval Academy, MD, 1970	#14
9. Brian Moynihan	Bank of America CEO since 2010	Brown University, RI, 1981	#15
10. Alan Mulally	Ford Motors CEO	University of	#101

	since 2006	Kansas, 1969	

Analysis: Of the 10 CEOs, 60% (six) attended and graduated from one of the top 50 colleges.

Presumptive conclusion: Attending one of the top-ranked 50 colleges appears to give a student a better chance to sit in the command position at a big company.

14.9. Closing thoughts on the role of college education in one's success in life.

College is such a brief moment in a life and many other factors are important to success. Personal traits, learning skills, motivation, and determination may make the real difference for a person's success. These traits are formed during high school years and are usually solidified during college time. The college dropouts hall of fame (www.collegedropoutshalloffame.com) includes many familiar names, including business successes Bill Gates, Larry Ellison, and Steve Jobs, as well as movie stars including Woody Alan, Tom Cruise, and Jennifer Aniston. These people did not finish or attended college yet are highly regarded as successful. But, as Bill Gates once advised college students: "Do not drop out of college unless you have a better idea than mine." After all, the list of successful college graduates is likely much longer than the list of successful dropouts.

So, why try to attend an Ivy or Ivy-like college? Well, these highly selective colleges typically have a long educational history, and have well established philosophies and traditions. They have tried and perfected their teaching system. With the highly competitive student body, a would-be-successful student is pushed to a higher level of probability of success after graduating from these colleges. These institutions should sharpen those critical factors of learning skills, motivation, and determination. As parents, we wish for our children to grow to adulthood with secure employment, a decent income, and a happy life. This conservative goal is more realistic and achievable if we help our children aim to attend an esteemed college.

Parents, have confidence in your students.

Help them achieve.

Then, celebrate your successful parenting.

After Words

My family and I are blessed. I am grateful to Lauda and Shaudi for their patience and for their tolerance to June's and my parental "tough love." I thank them for making my life full.

Lauda is doing well in medical school and calls me periodically with questions regarding hematological and oncological answers, especially before and after tests. He is taking one year off to pursue laboratory research funded by a grant he earned from the Howard Hugh Medical Institute.

Shaudi is "very busy" at Pomona College. He was supposed to call home every Sunday night, which he did for the first month. Subsequently, he became "too busy to call." He is on the school's ultimate Frisbee junior varsity team, he ran for student body office, and he tutors local high school students on Saturdays. At the end of his freshman year, he got all A's except one B+. He has not decided on a future career.

I am so lucky to have found June during our medical school years and to have married her. She is the most dedicated mother and wife. She has accompanied me along the journey of my career and of our children's rearing. She runs the household. I attribute much of the success of our children and of my career to her wisdom. She still provides free "private college counselor" advice for many of our family friends.

June believes I am suffering empty nest syndrome and am getting old by looking to the past in writing this book. I disagree. I believe our family experience captured a snapshot of a common experience of our generation: sweet joy in having children and bitter labor in rearing them, working hard to earn a living in the profession we chose, and dedication in serving others. I think parents in our generation are more involved and caring than our parents' generation, either in a home country or in the United States. Whether the increased involvement exerts a positive or negative influence on our offspring or on society will be determined by future generations.

I am also grateful to many of our family friends in providing encouragement for me to initiate this book and for sharing some of their experience. I often think of and pray for my extended family in China for shouldering the hardship so that I could do what I do today and write this book.

Many of my colleagues at work, in particular, Renee Yanke ARNP, AOCN; Linda Jacobsen RN, AOCN; and Lori Daveport, LPN, Don Miller RN, AOCN, provided me with some great suggestions. I thank them for their enthusiasm and for making the work environment more enjoyable.

Stephanie Haskins and her team also had some good feedback for me to incorporate in the text.

Dr. Patricia Bloom (PhD) was extremely generous by taking time off from her own book to coach me in book publishing and by editing the very first draft.

Some of the names listed above are patients of mine. I thank them and all of my patients for being my life teachers. It is their need that gives me a purpose of life. It is their life that makes my life full. It is their courage in facing cancer therapies that gets me through some difficult times of my own. It is their love of life that motivates me work hard. It is their supportive family that makes me better appreciate more my own. As mentioned in the book, I have a small "tear sac" that easily spills, and I share the spilling moments frequently with my patients and their families when we face decisions on life or death. It is by working with them that I learn the meaning of life and better appreciate the time and health I have.

Last but not least, I thank Robin Rothberg for her superb content editing and Jennifer Blakely for her meticulous copy editing.

References

1. Jonathan R. Cole: The Great American University: Its Rise to Preeminence, Its Indispensable National Role, Why It Must Be Protected. 2009. Public Affairs, Perseus Books Group.

2. Amy Chue: Battle Hymn of The Tiger Mother. 2011. The Penguin Press.

3. Elizabeth Wissner-Gross: What colleges do not tell you (and other parents do not want you to know): 272 secrets for getting your kid into the top school. 2006. Hudson Street Press.

4. College Essays that made a difference. By The Princeton Review, 2003. Princeton Review Publishing INC.

5. Katherine Cohen: Rock Hard Application: How to write a killer college application. 2003. Hyperion Publishing, NY

6. Katherine Cohen: The Truth About Getting In. 2002. Hyperion Publishing, NY

7. Andrew Ferguson: CRAZY U: one Dad's crash course in getting his kid into college. 2011, Publisher- Simon and Schuster.

8. Edward B Fiske and Bruce G Hammond: The Fiske Guide to College. 2010. Sourcebooks, INC

9. The best 376 colleges, 2012 edition (college admission guide). 2011. Princeton College Review INC

10. Ultimate College Guide by US News and World report. 2011 Edition. Publisher SOURCEBOOKS.

Appendix 1. The Common Application Form – detailed version

2011-12 First-year Application

For Spring 2012 or Fall 2012 Enrollment

APPLICANT

Legal Name_____

Preferred name, if not first name (only one) __   Former last name(s) ____

Birth Date __ Female _ Male   US Social Security Number, if any _____

Preferred Telephone _ Home _ Cell Home (_) ____ Cell (__) _____

E-mail Address _____ IM Address _____

Permanent home address _____

If different from above, please give your current mailing address for all admission correspondence. (from _____ to _____)

Current mailing address _____

If your current mailing address is a boarding school, include name of school here:
_____

FUTURE PLANS

Your answers to these questions will vary for different colleges. If the online system did not ask you to answer some of the questions you see in this section, this college chose not to ask that question of its applicants.

College _____ Deadline _____

Entry Term: _Fall (Jul-Dec) _Spring (Jan-Jun)

Decision Plan_____

Academic Interests _____

Career Interest_____

Do you intend to apply for need-based financial aid? _ Yes _ No

Do you intend to apply for merit-based scholarships? _ Yes _ No

Do you intend to be a full-time student?   _ Yes _ No

Do you intend to enroll in a degree program your first year? _Yes _No

Do you intend to live in college housing? _____

What is the highest degree you intend to earn? _____

DEMOGRAPHICS

Citizenship Status _____

Non-US Citizenship _____

Birthplace _____

Years lived in the US? _____ Years lived outside the US? _____

Language Proficiency (Check all that apply.) _____ S R W F H

Optional The items with a gray background are optional. No information you provide will be used in a discriminatory manner.

Religious Preference _____

US Armed Services veteran status _____

1. Are you Hispanic/Latino? _ Yes, Hispanic or Latino (including Spain) _ No

If yes, please describe your background_____

2. Regardless of your answer to the prior question, please indicate how you identify yourself. (Check one or more and describe your background.)

_ American Indian or Alaska Native (including all Original Peoples of the Americas)

   Are you Enrolled? _ Yes _ No

If yes, please enter Tribal Enrollment Number _____

_ Asian (including Indian subcontinent and Philippines)

_ Black or African American (including Africa and Caribbean)

_ Native Hawaiian or Other Pacific Islander (Original Peoples)

_ White (including Middle Eastern)

FAMILY

Please list both parents below, even if one or more is deceased or no longer has legal responsibilities toward you. Many colleges collect this information for demographic purposes even if you are an adult or an emancipated minor. If you are a minor with a legal guardian (an individual or government entity), then please list that information below as well. If you wish, you may list step-parents and/or other adults with whom you reside, or who otherwise care for you, in the Additional Information section.

Household

Parents' marital status (relative to each other): _ Never Married _ Married _ Civil Union/Domestic Partners _ Widowed _ Separated _ Divorced (date _____)

With whom do you make your permanent home? _ Parent 1 _ Parent 2 _ Both _ Legal Guardian _ Ward of the Court/State _ Other

If you have children, how many? _____

Legal Guardian (if other than a parent)

Relationship to you _____

Country of birth _____

Home address if different from yours_____

Preferred Telephone: _ Home _ Cell _ Work (____) _____

E-mail _____

Occupation _____

Employer _____

College (if any) _____ CEEB _____

Degree _____ Year _____

Graduate School (if any) _____ CEEB _____

Degree _____ Year _____

Siblings

Please give names and ages of your brothers or sisters. If they are enrolled in grades K-12 (or international equivalent), list their grade levels. If they have attended or are currently attending college, give the names of the undergraduate institution, degree earned, and approximate dates of attendance. If more than three siblings, please list them in the Additional Information section.

_____

Name Age & Grade Relationship

College Attended _____ CEEB _____

Degree earned _____ Dates _____

or expected *mm/yyyy – mm/yyyy*_____

Name Age & Grade Relationship

College Attended _____ CEEB _____

Degree earned _____ Dates _____

or expected *mm/yyyy – mm/yyyy*_____

Parent 1: _ Mother _ Father _ Unknown

Is Parent 1 living? _ Yes _ No (Date Deceased _____)

_____

Last/Family/Sur First/Given Middle Title (Mr./Mrs./Ms./Dr.)

Country of birth _____

Home address if different from yours _____

Preferred Telephone: _ Home _ Cell _ Work (_____) _____

E-mail _____

Occupation _____

Employer _____

College (if any) _____ CEEB _____

Degree _____ Year _____

Graduate School (if any) _____ CEEB _____

Degree _____ Year _____

Parent 2: _ Mother _ Father _ Unknown

Is Parent 2 living? _ Yes _ No (Date Deceased_____)

_____

Last/Family/Sur First/Given Middle Title (Mr./Mrs./Ms./Dr.)

Country of birth _____

Home address if different from yours_____

Preferred Telephone: _ Home _ Cell _ Work (____) _____

E-mail _____

Occupation _____

Employer _____

College (if any) _____ CEEB _____

Degree _____ Year _____

Graduate School (if any) _____ CEEB _____

Degree _____ Year _____

EDUCATION

Secondary Schools

Most recent secondary school attended _____Entry Date _____ Graduation Date

_____

School Type: _ Public _ Charter _ Independent _ Religious _ Home School

Address _____ CEEB/ACT Code _____

Counselor's Name _____Counselor's Title _____

E-mail _____ Telephone (___) ____ Fax (_____) _____

List all other secondary schools you have attended since 9th grade, including summer schools or enrichment programs hosted on a secondary school campus:

School Name & CEEB/ACT Code Location (City, State/Province, ZIP/Postal Code, Country) Dates Attended (mm/yyyy)

_____

Community program/Organization._____

If your education was or will be interrupted, please indicate so here:

_____

Colleges & Universities: Report all college attendance (including online) since 9th grade and indicate as College Course (CO) or Enrichment Program (EP) hosted on a college campus.

College/University Name & CEEB/ACT Code Location (City, State/Province, ZIP/Postal Code, Country) Degree Candidate? CO EP Dates Attended Degree Earned

Yes No mm/yyyy – mm/yyyy

_____ _____ _____

Were you issued a transcript for any work listed above? _ Yes _ No If yes, please have an official transcript sent as soon as possible.

ACADEMICS

The self-reported information in this section is not intended to take the place of your official records. Please note the requirements of each institution to which you are applying and arrange for official transcripts and score reports to be sent from your secondary school and the appropriate testing agencies. Where "Best Scores" are requested, please report the highest individual scores you have earned so far, even if those scores are from different test dates.

Grades: Class Rank _____ Class Size _____ Weighted? _ Yes _ No

GPA _____Scale _____ Weighted? _ Yes _ No

ACT Exam Dates: _____ Best Scores: _____ _____

(past & future) COMP mm/yyyy   English mm/yyyy   Math mm/yyyy

_____ _____

Reading mm/yyyy   Science mm/yyyy   Writing mm/yyyy

SAT Exam Dates: _____ Best Scores: ___ _____

(past & future)   Critical Reading mm/yyyy   Math mm/yyyy   Writing mm/yyyy

TOEFL/IELTS Exam Dates: _____Best Score: ____ ___ _____

(past & future) mm/yyyy mm/yyyy (so far) Test Score mm/yyyy

AP/IB

Subjects   Best Scores: _____

(per subject, so far) mm/yyyy Type & Subject Score

Current Courses Please indicate title, level (AP, IB, advanced honors, etc.) and credit value of all courses you are taking this year. Indicate quarter classes taken in the same semester on the appropriate semester line.

Full Year/First Semester/First Trimester Second Semester/Trimester Third Trimester *or additional first/second term courses if more space is needed*

_____

Honors Briefly list any academic distinctions or honors you have received since the 9th grade or international equivalent (e.g., National Merit, Cum Laude Society).

S(School) S/R(State or Regional N(National) I(International)

Grade level or post-graduate (PG): 9 10 11 12 PG S S/R N I

Honor: _____

Highest Level of Recognition: _____

EXTRACURRICULAR ACTIVITIES & WORK EXPERIENCE

Extracurricular Please list your principal extracurricular, volunteer, and work activities in their order of importance to you. Feel free to group your activities and paid work experience separately if you prefer. Use the space available to provide details of your activities and accomplishments (specific events, varsity letter, musical instrument, employer, etc.). To allow us to focus on the highlights of your activities, please complete this section even if you plan to attach a résumé.

Grade level or post-graduate (PG)_ 9 10 11 12 PG Hours

Approximate time spent ____ When did you participate in the activity?_____

Positions held___, honors won____, letters earned_____, or employer If applicable,

do you plan to participate in college?

WRITING

Please briefly elaborate on one of your extracurricular activities or work experiences in the space below.

_____

Please write an essay of 250 – 500 words on a topic of your choice or on one of the options listed below, and attach it to your application before submission. Please indicate your topic by checking the appropriate box. This personal essay helps us become acquainted with you as a person and student, apart from courses, grades, test scores, and other objective data. It will also demonstrate your ability to organize your thoughts and express yourself. *NOTE: Your Common Application essay should be the same for all colleges. Do not customize it in any way for individual colleges. Colleges that want customized essay responses will ask for them on*

a supplement form.

_ _ Evaluate a significant experience, achievement, risk you have taken, or ethical dilemma you have faced and its impact on you.

_ _ Discuss some issue of personal, local, national, or international concern and its importance to you.

_ _ Indicate a person who has had a significant influence on you, and describe that influence.

_ _ Describe a character in fiction, a historical figure, or a creative work (as in art, music, science, etc.) that has had an influence on you, and explain that influence.

_ _ A range of academic interests, personal perspectives, and life experiences adds much to the educational mix. Given your personal background, describe an experience that illustrates what you would bring to the diversity in a college community or an encounter that demonstrated the importance of diversity to you.

_ _ Topic of your choice.

Additional Information Please attach a separate sheet if you wish to provide details of circumstances or qualifications not reflected in the application.

Disciplinary History

_ Have you ever been found responsible for a disciplinary violation at any educational institution you have attended from the 9th grade (or the international equivalent) forward, whether related to academic misconduct or behavioral misconduct, that resulted in a disciplinary action? These actions could include, but are not limited to: probation, suspension, removal, dismissal, or expulsion from the institution.

_ Yes _ No

_ Have you ever been adjudicated guilty or convicted of a misdemeanor, felony, or other crime? _ Yes _ No

[Note that you are not required to answer "yes" to this question, or provide an explanation, if the criminal adjudication or conviction has been expunged, sealed, annulled, pardoned, destroyed, erased, impounded, or otherwise ordered by a court to be kept confidential.] If you answered "yes" to either or both questions, please attach a separate sheet of paper that gives the approximate date of each incident, explains the circumstances, and reflects on what you learned from the experience. Note: Applicants are expected to immediately notify the institutions to which they are applying should there be any changes to the information requested in this application, including disciplinary history.

SIGNATURE

214

Application Fee Payment: If this college requires an application fee, how will you be paying it?

_ Online Payment _Will Mail Payment _ Online Fee Waiver Request _Will Mail Fee Waiver Request

Required Signature

I certify that all information submitted in the admission process—including the application, the personal essay, any supplements, and any other supporting materials—is my own work, factually true, and honestly presented, and that these documents will become the property of the institutions to which I am applying and will not be returned to me. I understand that I may be subject to a range of possible disciplinary actions, including admission revocation, expulsion, or revocation of course credit, grades, and degree, should the information I have certified be false.

I acknowledge that I have reviewed the application instructions for each college receiving this application. I understand that all offers of admission are conditional, pending receipt of final transcripts showing work comparable in quality to that upon which the offer was based, as well as honorable dismissal from the school.

I affirm that I will send an enrollment deposit (or equivalent) to only one institution; sending multiple deposits (or equivalent) may result in the withdrawal of my admission offers from all institutions. [Note: students may send an enrollment deposit (or equivalent) to a second institution where they have been admitted from the waitlist, provided that they inform the first institution that they will no longer be enrolling.]

Signature _____

Date _____

Appendix 2. College Planning and Application Time Table

Grade Level	Extracurricular Activities	Goal
Before 5th	1. Cultivate interests in books and good study habit 2. Set limits on playtime 3. Try varieties of activities: arts, sports, music, et al	1. A good study habit goes for a life time 2. Learn parental expectations 3. Find out where the interest and talent lays
7th - 8th	1. Sports, arts — narrow down to one each. 2. Prepare for and take the real SAT I or ACT for practice.	1. Join a team, club or arts group 2. Participate in university sponsored summer camps
9th - 10th	1. Sports, arts – join school team or group 2. Volunteer, in or out of school 3. Spend summers on domestic or international volunteer work 4. Prepare for PSAT and SAT I	1. Earn a team leadership position 2. Earn an official position in a club 3. Accumulate hours and collect material for college essays 4. Ace PSAT to qualify to be a National Merit Scholar semi-finalist.
11th 1st semester (Fall and Winter)	1. Sports, arts – continue school team or group 2. Volunteer, in or out of school 3. Take the real PSAT 4. SAT I preparation: class or self-study 5. SAT II preparation: class or self-study.	1. Continue team leadership position 2. Continue club official position 3. Accumulate hours and collect material for college essay 4. Write an essay to compete to be a National Merit Scholar finalist 5. Ace SAT I on the first attempt 6. Ace SAT II on the first attempt
11th 2nd semester (Spring)	1. Sports, arts – continue school team or group 2. Volunteer, in or out of school 3. Take SAT I in April, May or June 4. Take the SAT II subject tests	1. Continue team leadership position 2. Continue club official position 3. Accumulate hours and collect material for college essay 4. If needed, make multiple test attempts for best combined score

	5. Interview and find a private college counselor, if desired	5. Prepare for college application
Summer between 11th-12th	1. Draft long essay for college applications 2. Compile college list via online research 3. Continue summer volunteer work	1. Be prepared for a long haul 2. Sign up for fall season college campus tours 3. Spend three summers on the same activity; it shows compassion and perseverance.
12th (September, October, November)	1. Continue to retake SAT I or II if scores are not at desired level 2. Make college campus visits, if affordable 3. Ask teachers and counselors for recommendation letters (mid to late September) 4. Continue to work on the long essay for college applications 5. Get the class rank and GPA from the school counselor 6. Work on short college essay for the early decision or action college	1. SAT I total score should be at least 2200; SAT II should be at least 720 2. Narrow the list to nine colleges 3. Get favorite teachers' promises to write recommendations 4. Perfect the essay, after many edits 5. Set up application account via www.commonapp.org 6. Take early decision or early action decisions/options seriously
12th (December, January)	1. Meet deadlines: December 1 or January 1 for most early applications 2. Continue to work on short essays in case early application fails to secure an admission letter	1. Check college web site or email for announcement of early admission decisions
12th (January, February)	1. If early application failed, apply to other colleges. If it succeeded, pay the deposit and skip to activities for May, June. 2. Watch deadlines; each college requires materials	1. Choose three dream colleges; three reachable colleges and three safety colleges 2. Aim to submit applications one week before a deadline

	by different dates and times	
12th (February, March)	1. Prepare for alumni interviews: research the college; be genuinely interested in the college 2. Monitor accounts at each college applied to for any missing document.	1. Connect well with the alumni interviewer to earn a glowing evaluation report 2. Submit any missing document promptly, incomplete files will not be read
12th (March, April)	1. Anxiously await good news; check email and regular mailbox 2. Provide supplemental information to waitlist colleges	1. Take action promptly, if waitlisted 2. Get off the waitlist to land a spot at a dream college
12th (April, May)	1. If unsure where to attend, revisit colleges that offered admission 2. Pay deposit to the best college	1. Select a final dream college to attend 2. College admission secured!
12th (May, June)	1. Celebrate successful high school life and parenting 2. Enjoy time with high school friends, as the group will soon be apart	1. Appreciate hard work – it pays off 2. Cultivate friendships, and continue loyalty to high school friends.
12th (July, August)	1. Shop for college-bound student 2. Choose 1st year courses in college	1. Ensure functional living away from home 2. Try to listen to parents.
12th (August, September)	1. Send student off to college 2. Reflect on college application journey.	1. Keep parental love active from afar 2. Treat parental "empty nest syndrome" 3. Help other parents achieve what you have done.

Appendix 3. The 51 Tips and 7 facts/fictions in Dream College Admissions Made Possible

Chapter 2:
- Tip: A student should take classes in middle school to qualify for high-level classes in high school.
- Tip: A student should take as many high level classes as he or she can achieve good grades in.
- Tip: A student should take an extra course, online or through a community college, to increase weighted class rank.
- Tip: Most children need parental "tough love" to kick them into high gear, academically.

Chapter 3:
- Tip: A student should register early to take the SAT at the location closest to home.
- Tip: Use a consistent home study method to work with your child to improve what you expect to be his or her weakest subject areas on the SAT I.
- Tip: Early enrichment classes can pay dividends years later.
- Tip: For special benefits, and to best prepare for the real exam, a student should take a practice SAT I test before high school.
- Tip: If parents feel they cannot help a student improve in a subject area, consider hiring a private tutor, but ensure the student still makes progress.
- Tip: To be most impressive to colleges, a student should ace the SAT I on the first attempt.
- Tip: If a student isn't sufficiently motivated, try offering an affordable incentive to reward a test score that reaches a certain number.
- Tip: Books are important, but experience can also form a quality education.
- Tip: If trying to choose between the SAT I and ACT, let a student take a simulation of each exam to determine which score starts out higher.

Chapter 4:
- Tip: Academically inclined peers can help keep a high school student on track, especially if they take challenging classes together.

Chapter 5:
- Tip: Parents should help students learn about and enter competitions, since honors and awards can garner positive attention from college admissions officers.

- Tip: Even if an attempt doesn't lead to an award or honor, help your child find value in lessons learned, and possibly apply those lessons elsewhere on the college application.

Chapter 6:
- Tip: Don't let a student study so much that he or she doesn't have time to cultivate friends or outside interests.
- Tip: Nurture, then help your child display talent in a sector of the arts or sports via a school group, regional organization, or even national stage.
- Tip: A student should find a school club to join, then mature into an officer role.
- Tip: Your student can't find a compelling school club? He or she should create one!
- Tip: Make a larger impact by consolidating humanitarian into one or two consistent activities, plus international work, if possible.
- Tip: To best benefit the community in need, volunteer work should stem from a student's interests.
- Tip: Beyond college applications, volunteer work should help students become better people and more appreciative of their own good fortune.

Chapter 7:
- Tip: Once test scores and high school grades are the best they can be, essays can make the admissions difference for a range of students.
- Tip: The best essays are narratives that show the admissions officer how the student is a living, breathing person, not just a compilation of test scores and high school grades.
- Tip: Once a student finds an appropriate essay topic, it will probably take many drafts to produce his or her best work.
- Tip: The short essay demands research, enthusiasm, facts showing how a student can benefit a college, not vice-versa.
- Tip: Some students feign interest in a less popular major to gain admission into a larger university. This is unwise, and often easily detectable to an experienced admissions officer.

Chapter 8:
- Tip: The best – and most valued – recommendation letters come from people who worked closely enough with a student to truly get to know him or her.
- Tip: Early in his or her senior year, a student should ask a favorite teacher for a recommendation letter. If the teacher agrees, write examples to help remind the teacher of specific, quality interactions.

Chapter 9:
- Tip: A student should get to know his or her high school guidance counselor, often an overburdened worker who holds much responsibility and power.
- Tip: If the family can afford it, a private college counselor can help enforce deadlines and gently push students in ways a parent sometimes cannot.

Chapter 10:
- Tip: A few weeks before a campus visit, sign up online for a group tour. A reservation ensures a preview of the school at a preferred time, on a preferred day.
- Tip: A campus visit can motivate a student, and the student's name in the tour log can assure an admissions officer of the student's intention to enroll.
- Tip: On campus tours, a parent may have specific concerns, such as classes and programs. A student, by contrast, may soak up the general atmosphere, intuitively trying to figure out if this type of school best fits his or her personality.
- Tip: The statistics in college reference books and guides can help determine what tier a college is for a student: dream, reachable, or safety net. Apply to more than one of each.

Chapter 11:
- Tip: Printing application forms helps students see their information the same way admissions officers will eventually read it.
- Tip: It can be easier to earn acceptance to a competitive university by strategically and ethically using early application or early decision applications.
- Tip: Instead of relaxing, early applicants should continue to draft short essays for other schools.

Chapter 12:

- Tip: After the application is in, a parent should ensure a student checks all accounts a college or university could use to update the application's status.
- Tip: Alumni interviews are for borderline applicants. Students should take them seriously.
- Tip: Practice for the before, during, and after of alumni interviews provides a lifelong benefit.
- Tip: Don't count on admission from a wait list.

Chapter 13:

- Tip: Even if their experience differs from yours, if your budget can afford it, help your children enjoy the fun of high school and, later, of college.
- Tip: If the household includes a younger child or children, keep in mind their needs as the older sibling prepares to leave for college.
- Tip: Dog is the best friend of man: having a dog can ease family tension during college application, soothe your student's stress and may improve your student's academic performance.
- Tip: Enjoy the chance to buy the things your soon-to-be collegian will need or want at school.
- Tip: For moving-in day, use or rent a large enough car to handle the load from shopping.
- Tip: To get the best location of the bed, arrive early at the dormitory: all colleges have the policy of "first come, first grab.
- Tip: Your emotions may surprise you on move-in day. Let them flow.
- Tip: As you cram your car full of your student's belongings, be sure to keep a corner of your glove compartment open for a box of tissues for the parents.

Chapter 14:

- 90% of the most influential Americans attended or graduated from the top 50 colleges.
- 90% of the top Oncologists attended or graduated from the top 50 colleges.
- 80% of the recent Americans Nobel Laureates attended or graduated from the top 50 colleges.
- 70% of the last ten US Presidents attended or graduated from the top 50 colleges.
- 60% of the top CEO's attended or graduated from the top 50 colleges.
- 50% of the richest Americans attended or graduated from the top 50 colleges.
- 30% of the US Congressional leaders attended or graduated from the top 50 colleges.

Appendix 4. About the Author

Dr. Peter Jiang is a proud father of two hard working college students. He is a cancer specialist presently working in a cancer center in Everett, WA. He also holds a clinical faculty position at the University of Washington School of Medicine and enjoys teaching medical doctoral students. He likes hiking and running with the family goldendoodle.

Other publications by Dr. Jiang:

Books:

1. Allogeneic Immunotherapy for Malignant Diseases. 2000. Publisher: Marcel Dekker, Inc. New York. (co-editor).
2. Graft Versus Leukemia Reactivity After Allogeneic Bone Marrow Transplantation in Man. 1991. PhD Thesis. Medical Library, University of London, UK.

Peer reviewed research articles (only the 1st and 2nd authorship listed here):

1. MacDonald D, Jiang YZ, et al: Recombinant interleukin 2 for acute myeloid leukemia in first Complete Remission: a pilot study. Leukemia Research 1990; 14:967-973.
2. Jiang YZ, Kanfer E, et al: Graft versus leukemia effect following allogeneic bone marrow transplantation: emergence of cytotoxic T lymphocytes to host leukemia cells. Bone Marrow Transplantation 1991; 14:253-258.
3. MacDonald D, Jiang YZ, et al: Acute myeloid leukemia relapsing following interleukin-2 treatment expresses the alpha chain of the interleukin-2 receptor. British Journal of Haematology 1991; 77:43-49.

4. Jiang YZ, MacDonald M, et al: Is graft-versus leukemia effect separable from graft-versus host reactivity? Bone Marrow Transplantation 1991; 7(2):26.

5. Cullis JO, Jiang YZ, et al: Donor leukocyte infusion in the treatment of chronic myeloid leukemia in relapse following allogeneic bone marrow transplantation. Blood 1992; 79:1379-81.

6. Barrett AJ, and Jiang YZ: Review: Immune response to chronic myeloid leukemia. Bone Marrow Transplantation 1992; 9:305-311.

7. Schwarer AP, Jiang YZ, et al: Frequency of anti-recipient alloreactive helper T-cell precursors in donor blood and graft versus host disease after HLA-identical sibling bone marrow transplantation. Lancet 1993:341:203-205.

8. Jiang YZ, Cullis JO, et al: T cell and NK cell mediated graft versus leukemia reactivity following donor buffy coat transfusion to treat relapse after marrow transplantation for chronic myeloid leukemia. Bone Marrow Transplantation 1993:11:133-138.

9. Schwarer AP, Jiang YZ, et al: Comparison of helper and cytotoxic anti-recipient T cell frequencies in unrelated bone marrow transplantation. Transplantation 1994:58:1198-1203.

10. Jiang YZ, Barrett AJ: Cellular and cytokine mediated effects of CD4+ lymphocyte lines generated in vitro against chronic myelogenous leukemia. Experimental Hematology 1995; 23:1167-1172.

11. Mavroudis DA, Jiang YZ, et al: Selective depletion of alloreactivity against haplotype mismatched related individuals: A new approach to GVHD prophylaxis in haploidentical bone marrow Transplantation. Bone Marrow Transplantation 1996, 17:793-799.

12. Jiang YZ, Couriel D, et al: Interaction of NK cells with MHC class II: Reversal of HLA-DR1 mediated protection of K562 transfectant from NK cell-mediated cytolysis by brefeldin-A. Immunology 1996, 87:481-486.

13. Jiang YZ, Mavroudis DA, et al: Alloreactive CD4+T lymphocytes can exert cytotoxicity to CML cells processing and presenting exogenous antigen. British Journal of Hematology 1996,93:606-612.

14. Jiang YZ, Barrett AJ, et al: Association of Natural Killer cell immune recovery with a graft-vs.-leukemia effect independent of graft vs. host disease following allogeneic bone marrow transplantation. Annals of Hematology 1996, 74:1-6.

15. Jiang YZ, Mavroudis DA, et al: Preferential T cell receptor (TCR) V-beta usage by allogeneic T cell against myeloid leukemia cells: Implications for separating GVL and GVHD. Bone Marrow Transplantation 1997, 19:899-903

16. Jiang YZ, Barrett AJ: Review: Allogeneic CD4+T lymphocyte immune responses to chronic myelogenous leukemia. Leukemia and Lymphoma 1997, 28:33-42.

17. Weichold F, Jiang YZ, et al: Regulation of a graft vs leukemia effect by major histocompatability complex class II Molecules on leukemia cells: HLA-DR1 expression renders K562 cell tumors Resistant to adoptively transferred lymphocytes in severe combined immuno-deficiency/non-obese diabetic mice. Blood 1997, 90:4553-8.

18. Hoshino T, Jiang YZ, et al: Transfection of IL12 cDNA into tumor cells induces cytotoxic immune responses against native tumor: implications for tumor vaccination. Cancer Gene Therapy 1998; 5:150-7.

19. Molldrem JJ, Jiang YZ, et al: Haematological response of patients with myelodysplastic syndrome to anti-thymocyte globulin is associated with a loss of lymphocyte-mediated inhibition of CFU-GM and alterations in T-cell receptor V-beta profiles. British Journal of Haematology 1998, 102(5): 1314-22.

20. Van Rhee F, Jiang YZ, et al: Human G- CSF-mobilized CD34-positive peripheral blood progenitor cells can stimulate allogeneic T-cell responses:

implications for graft rejection in mismatched trans-plantation. British Journal of Haematology 1999, 105(4): 1014-24.

21. Jiang YZ, Hutchinson K, et al: Thyroid storm presenting as multiple organ dysfunction syndrome. Chest 2000; 118(3):877-9.

22. Deeg HJ, Jiang PYZ, et al: Hematologic response of patients with MDS to ATG/etanercept correlate with improved flow scores of marrow cells. Leukemia Research 2004, 28:1177-80

23. Jiang PYZ, Renee Yanke, et al: A Novel Effective Therapy for Refractory Angiosarcoma of the face and scalp. Advances in Clinical Hematology and Oncology 2011; 9:502-4.

Made in United States
Troutdale, OR
07/11/2023

11139507R00148